Easter

BEHOLD YOUR KING

LIFEWAY WOMEN

LifeWay Press®
Nashville, Tennessee

Published by LifeWay Press® • © 2020 LifeWay Christian Resources • Nashville, TN

ISBN: 978-1-0877-1572-8 • Item: 005826669
Dewey decimal classification: 263.93
Subject headings: EASTER / HOLY WEEK / JESUS CHRIST--MESSIAHSHIP

To order additional copies of this resource, write to LifeWay Church Resources Customer Service; One LifeWay Plaza; Nashville, TN 37234; order online at *www.lifeway.com;* fax 615.251.5933; phone toll free 800.458.2772; or email *orderentry@lifeway.com.*

Printed in the United States of America

Adult Ministry Publishing • LifeWay Church Resources • One LifeWay Plaza • Nashville, TN 37234

EDITORIAL TEAM, LIFEWAY WOMEN PUBLISHING

Becky Loyd
Director, LifeWay Women

Tina Boesch
Manager, LifeWay Women Bible Studies

Sarah Doss
Editorial Project Leader, LifeWay Women Bible Studies

Mike Wakefield
Content Editor

Jennifer Siao
Production Editor

Lauren Ervin
Graphic Designer

Contents

How to Use This Study

Welcome! This Easter study may vary from others you've done. We know many Bible study groups don't always meet during the Easter season, so we wanted to provide a study you can do alone, with family, or with your friends! Along with daily personal study, we've provided activities each week you may choose to do by yourself, with your kids, or with friends. Each week you'll find:

- an introduction;
- group discussion questions in the Group Guide;
- five days of personal study;
- activities to do individually, with kids and teens, or with your friends and family.

Use the five days of personal study to reflect, allowing God's Word to nourish your soul. This study is designed to help you see the true meaning of Easter—that our hope is found only in Jesus Christ, the risen Savior.

GROUP DISCUSSION

If you decide to do this study with others, use the Group Guide discussion questions and the personal study each week to guide your conversation. In addition to answering the questions in the Group Guide, invite women to share specific things they learned from each day of study and to share Scripture that made an impact on them during the week. During the group meeting you may want to invite women to share how they've incorporated the kids, teens, and adult activities into this Easter season. As an option, your group may want to bring the supplies needed to complete one of the activities in a group setting as you discuss the Group Guide questions and personal study.

Because Easter can be a busy season, we hope the activities in the study provide a time of rest and reflection. We hope you'll enjoy sharing the love of Jesus with your family, friends, and neighbors during this time of the year.

A GROUP TIME MIGHT LOOK SOMETHING LIKE THIS:

- Welcome everyone to the group.
- Discuss the questions on the Group Guide page for that week.
- Review the five days of personal study.
- Ask women to share any special activities they added to their week as they focused on Easter.
- Close in prayer.

SHARE WITH OTHERS

There may be those in your neighborhood or community who don't understand the meaning of Easter. Invite them to join you. Build authentic relationships with them. Use the Group Guide questions and host a group in your home to share what the Bible says about Jesus' death and resurrection and how your celebration of Easter is different because of Christ.

Introduction

Easter has become a part of the fabric of our culture, especially in the United States. Almost immediately after Valentine's Day, the life-size cupids succumb to aisles littered with bunnies, chicks, and pastels. Folks who wouldn't claim to be "religious" even celebrate Easter, popping a pack of PEEPS® into their carts on the way out of the store.

One of the reasons we love Easter is because, in many ways, it signals the long-awaited arrival of spring, bursting with new life and new hope, just when we think we can't handle the doldrums of winter one moment longer.

Many of us get wrapped up in the joys of the celebration and the extravagance of Easter services without understanding what it's actually all about. I think we'd all agree, Easter was a significant event—otherwise, why are we still marking the occasion thousands of years later? But do we really understand the deeper meaning?

That's the heart behind the study you hold in your hands. We want to take five weeks together to intentionally and prayerfully pull back the curtain, asking God to help us understand the big picture of Easter—surely everything we've learned in these Passion plays wasn't wrong—while also exploring some of the deeper meanings of what God was doing in Jesus' death and resurrection and the days leading up to these events.

WHERE WE'RE HEADED

Our main focus in this study will be on Passion Week—the last few days of Jesus' thirty-three years here on earth. We'll move chronologically through these days, watching Him purposefully and lovingly walk toward the cross. Then, we'll see Him resurrected, modeling new life, defeating fear of death and sin forever.

I think you'd agree, peoples' last actions and last words carry great weight. In the final moments of our lives, we only want to communicate the important things, the most true and pure things to the people we love most.

In exploring Passion Week, we are watching Jesus finish well. Being fully God as well as fully man, He knew His time was short. We will witness Him making sure He said what He needed to say to His family and followers whom He loved so dearly. We will see Jesus walk through the hardest assignment God the Father has ever handed out. We will watch Him suffer with unrelenting perseverance, integrity, and purpose.

We're going to unpack several of the Old Testament prophecies and how they were fulfilled in the last days of Jesus' life. We're going to examine some of the meaning and intention behind Jesus' activity during Passion Week. And we're going to see how Jesus' actions thousands of years ago speak directly to our everyday lives now and our eternal lives forever.

As we'll explore together, the first century world was languishing in pain and suffering and injustice, with no hope in sight. Jesus burst on the scene offering an "unorthodox" (pun intended) way to new life and joy—just when He knew we couldn't handle this world of darkness and hopelessness a moment longer. He sacrificed Himself on the cross, died, and rose again the third day to bring us inexhaustible purpose and unspeakable joy now and forever.

Jesus' suffering was meant to bring you new life. If you ask me, that's the best news there ever was.

Augustine is famously quoted as saying, "We are Easter people and alleluia is our song."[1] As followers of Jesus, understanding the beauty and importance of His sacrifice allows us each to add our voices to the alleluia chorus of worship that's been sung by believers throughout the ages—one that will be sung for all of eternity. A sacrifice of praise that's more than deserved for Jesus' spotless sacrifice for us. And while we're on this side of heaven, we are uniquely positioned to point others to Him as our glorious Savior and our mighty Lord.

We pray this study will fuel your joy and hope in being loved by Jesus. We pray it will spur you to intimate worship of Him. We pray it will lead you to tell others how Jesus came to save them too.

The chorus needs your alleluia. Let's start warming up our voices.

JESUS'
LAST WEEK

SUNDAY	MONDAY	TUESDAY	WEDNESDAY

- Royal entry into Jerusalem
  (Mark 11:1-10)

- Weeps over Jerusalem
  (Luke 19:41-44)

- Spends night at Bethany
  (Mark 11:11)

- Curses the fig tree
  (Matt. 21:18-22)

- Cleanses the temple
  (Mark 11:15-19)

- Teaches in parables
  (Matt. 21:28–22:14)

- Debates the rulers in the temple
  (Matt. 22:15-46)

- Mount of Olives discourse
  (Matt. 24–25)

- Anointed at Bethany
  (Mark 14:3-9)

- Betrayal plot is formed
  (Luke 22:1-6)

THURSDAY	FRIDAY	SATURDAY	SUNDAY

- The Passover meal
  (Luke 22:7-20)

- Trials in Jerusalem
  (Luke 22:66–23:25)

- In the tomb
  (Matt. 27:62-66)

- Resurrection
  (Luke 24:1-15)

- Washes disciples' feet
  (John 13:1-17)

- Crucifixion and burial
  (John 19:16-42)

- Intercessory prayer
  (John 17)

- Agony in Gethsemane
  (Matt. 26:36-46)

- Betrayal and arrest
  (Matt. 26:47-56)

Hope for Redemption

The Promised Messiah

by Sarah Doss

If you're familiar with Easter, you may have heard about Jesus' sacrifice on the cross for the sins of humankind and how He rose from the dead three days later. If you had to pick and choose, I'd say those are the most important "big headline" pieces of the Easter story—the crucial elements and, better still, key linchpins of the Christian faith. If you know those facts, you've got a leg up. Congrats.

But, in this introductory week, we want to look a little deeper, past the "highlights" and the chronology of the events of the week Jesus died on the cross. We want to journey back to the Old Testament to understand some of the history and prophecy that laid the groundwork for Jesus' appearance as Messiah. As we'll come to see, God spoke many beautiful Old Testament words of love that found their echo and fulfillment in Jesus—His life, death, and resurrection.

Though it sounds strange to our earthly ears, Jesus' sacrifice on the cross to save us from our sin wasn't a contingency plan that God was forced to put in place when Adam and Eve let us all down in the garden of Eden. In fact, that dark day on Golgotha was the plan all along.

Early in Scripture, we witness God masterfully sowing seeds of hope and redemption, casting shadows of the Messiah who would come. Admittedly, we have the benefit of reading the Old Testament from this side of the cross. Since we know who Jesus is and was—how He loved, how He acted, how He spoke to His followers and led with a servant's heart—it's much easier for us to see the Jesus-shaped holes in the Messianic references throughout the Old Testament.

But our brothers and sisters who lived in the Old Testament world didn't have such a luxury. They received these prophecies with great hope, but were only able to see them in part, unsure of what they were really being shown.

I imagine it almost as if they were looking through a kaleidoscope; they saw the beautiful shapes God might be placing together, but the edges were never quite clear and the image constantly shifting. Mesmerizing yet baffling. Who could imagine how it would all come together? Only God knew how all the pieces would lock into place to reveal the Savior whom we desperately needed.

And God, in His kindness, started giving us glimpses of who He was.

Almost immediately after Adam and Eve chose to do what was right in their own eyes, we hear God promise a Redeemer to come, One who would crush the serpent's head (Gen. 3:15). God points to the coming of Jesus in the Exodus story—the deliverance with the Passover and the sacrifice of a lamb. And He tells us of a coming Messiah who will appear as a servant, humbly suffering to help us.

As we look backward from the cross, I can't help but be struck by the care and intentionality of God in crafting a rescue for us, His wayward and helpless people, from the beginning. He illuminated each step of the way, gradually giving us shadows of Jesus along with grace and understanding bit by bit, pulling our hearts out of despair and buoying them with hope time and again. And He's still doing it.

We pray this week will fuel your worship of God as you see how intricately and beautifully Jesus fulfilled and fulfills all the promises God made to us all along.

Let's put ourselves in the sandals of our Old Testament brothers and sisters and marvel at the hope and light the coming Messiah brought with Him.

What's your favorite Easter tradition? How did you celebrate Easter growing up? How do you celebrate it now?

Do you think we can become numb to the Easter story? Explain. What can we do to experience Easter in a fresh way this year?

Have you ever been in what you felt like was a hopeless situation? Explain. Before Christ came, how was our spiritual situation hopeless?

Think of someone close to you who doesn't know Jesus. Do you think she considers her spiritual situation hopeless? Why or why not? If she were to ask you what's the big deal about Easter, how would you answer her?

Why did you choose to do this study? What do you hope to get out of it?

Take a moment to pray, asking God to help you walk through this Easter season with new eyes and a teachable heart. Also pray for the person close to you who doesn't know Christ. Pray for her heart to be tender to the gospel and that you would have the opportunity to talk with her about the meaning of Easter.

EASTER WAS THE PLAN BEFORE THE FOUNDATION OF THE WORLD

by Michelle R. Hicks

Read Genesis 3.

Have you ever put a plan in place to diet or exercise in order to lose weight? What were the results?

Women will try all kinds of things to lose weight. Sometimes we choose specific diets or exercise regimens. Other times we turn to certain vitamins or powders mixed with water before meals. We create meal plans and reorganize schedules to build in time for exercise. Millions (or billions) of dollars are spent each year on marketing products and services to dieters. The advertisers use before and after photos, claims of rapid weight loss, and sometimes the promise that no dieting or exercise is required at all. Believe me, I've been drawn in by many. How about you?

Sadly, I've discovered that some of these advertisements for weight-loss products and services are exaggerated claims or just false information mixed with a little truth. Giving into the temptation to hope and believe that the product will deliver the desired results often ends with disappointment and hopelessness. And that is where we begin our focus of Easter—temptation and the fall. It's a moment where dazzling promises were marketed using false information mixed with a little truth, but the result was devastating. Sin entered the world and with it came hopelessness. However, we also discover that God was not caught off guard. He had a plan crafted before the foundation of the world—the ultimate hope, a Savior. Jesus.

In the beginning God (Gen. 1:1). I love how the Bible starts with the focus and foundation on God. But it isn't long until Genesis 3 reveals the account of Eve being tempted and deceived by the serpent. Most of us are familiar with this beautiful beginning that turned into tragedy. Adam and Eve sinned by eating from the one and only tree God had forbidden. Genesis 3 reveals the curses and repercussions of sin that we describe as the fall.

Reread Genesis 3 and write a short summary of each passage.

Committing the sin (Gen. 3:1-8)

Confronting the sinners (Gen. 3:9-13)

Consequences of the sin (Gen. 3:14-24)

Ultimately, the consequence for sin is death, both physically and spiritually (Rom. 6:23). Eternal separation from God is the result. But God, in His goodness, had a plan from the beginning.

When the Lord was walking in the garden after Adam and Eve sinned, He came seeking those who were now lost. This loving act demonstrates how God loved us and had a plan in place for salvation. God came to seek and save humanity right from the start. His plan culminated in Jesus Christ—His death, burial, and resurrection.

How do we see a foreshadowing of that plan in Genesis 3:15?

Genesis 3:15 is often called the *protoevangelium*—the first gospel proclamation.[1] The hostility between Eve and her enemy, the serpent (later identified in Rev. 12:9 as Satan) is representative of the spiritual battle that continues to this day. Because of Adam's sin, we are all enslaved to sin and dead in our sins. We carry out the "inclinations of our flesh" and are "by nature children under wrath" (Eph. 2:1-3). In other words, we have no hope. But in Genesis 3:15, God told the serpent there was One coming from the woman's "offspring," who would "strike (his) head." To strike or crush the head of the snake is a picture of fatal and final destruction. That's what happened through Christ's coming to be our perfect sacrifice. Jesus has defeated death and Satan. Even in physical death we can have spiritual victory and eternal life because of the sacrificial work of Jesus Christ. Because of Easter.

Let's look at some additional verses that confirm God's plan for Easter—a plan for us to know the Savior.

READ THE FOLLOWING VERSES AND TAKE NOTES:	
ACTS 2:23	
ROMANS 5:12-21	
COLOSSIANS 1:19-22	
1 PETER 1:18-20	

How do these verses confirm God had a plan for our redemption before the foundation of the world?

Which ones are most meaningful to you? Why?

What do you need to be reminded of most this Easter?

Since all of humanity came from Adam, we are all subject to physical and spiritual death, which is the punishment for sin. As Paul said in Romans 3:23, all of us are sinners. We have all fallen short of the glory of God. If salvation and forgiveness for our sin depends on our goodness or our effort, we are not going to be saved. We might wish to be different but we do not have the power to change on our own. The separation that started in the garden of Eden was only able to be closed by the offspring of the woman, Jesus, the God-man, born of a virgin. What was a shadow in Genesis 3:15 became the Light of the world in Christ. Because of His death on the cross we can be made alive again (John 5:24) and experience eternal life (John 3:16-17).

Why do you celebrate Easter?

What traditions or activities do you take part in that remind you of Jesus' death, burial, and resurrection?

Read Romans 5:6-8 and write down what these verses mean to you.

We know there is a great, sovereign God and that we answer to Him, but we still rebel intentionally or mess up unintentionally. We understand what we should do, but we keep coming up short. It sounds hopeless. We are lost. But we are not hopeless because we have been found. What we could not do, God has done.

Just as God walked in the garden seeking Adam and Eve after they sinned, God seeks after us. Instead of expecting us to rise up to Him, He came down to us. He came to seek and save those who had been lost (Luke 19:10). If Genesis 3 did not happen, we wouldn't need Easter. But Easter was not God's plan B. It was God's sovereign plan all along.

PASSOVER FORESHADOWED A GREATER SACRIFICE

by Kailey Black

We often associate meals with our holiday celebrations. Turkey and dressing at Thanksgiving. Cinnamon rolls on Christmas morning. Hot dogs and bratwursts on the Fourth of July. My personal favorite is homemade apple pie for my birthday, which occurs during apple season in the fall.

When the Israelites left Egypt after 430 years of slavery, God introduced a new annual celebration: Passover. This meal consisted of a roasted lamb, bitter herbs, and unleavened bread. I'm not sure about you, but this menu doesn't sound quite so appetizing to me. However, God had a plan and a purpose for this special meal in the Israelites' history and beyond.

> What meals or traditions do you associate with holidays or annual celebrations? How do these traditions remind you of past events in your life?

Before we dive into the Passover story, let's rewind for a moment to the Book of Genesis. God made a covenant with Abram, soon-to-be Abraham. While God promised to make Abraham's descendants numerous, He also noted their future slavery in a foreign land.

Read Genesis 15:13-14.

Fast-forward through the stories of Abraham, Isaac, and Jacob, and the growth of the Israelite nation. Jacob's older sons sold their brother Joseph into slavery, which relocated him to Egypt. But with God's favor upon him, Joseph rose in status among the Egyptians. A famine later forced Jacob's sons to travel to Egypt, where the family reconciled and reunited under Joseph's elite status and care. After Joseph's death, however, all that changed.

Read Exodus 1:9-11.

These verses start the fulfillment of what God told Abraham in Genesis 15:13. Generation after generation of Israelites knew only slavery. This oppression continued for over four hundred years, but God did not forget His promise to Abraham. As Exodus 2:23-24 says, "The Israelites groaned because of their difficult labor, and they cried out, and their cry for help because of the difficult labor ascended to God. God heard their groaning, and God remembered his covenant with Abraham, with Isaac, and with Jacob." The use of "remembered" doesn't mean God forgot His promise, rather, it was now the time to honor it. [2]

Have you ever felt overlooked or forgotten by God? What were the circumstances?

In Exodus 3, God called Moses to advocate for the Israelites' freedom to Pharaoh, which Pharaoh refused to grant. Nine plagues then ravaged Egypt. But after each devastating event, Pharaoh's heart remained unchanged and he further oppressed the Israelites. Scripture details the tenth and final plague in Exodus 11—the death of the firstborn. But God had a plan for the Israelites.

Read Exodus 12:1-13 and summarize God's plan.

To prepare the Israelites for the night His destroyer would invade Egypt, God instituted Passover. Each Israelite household was to select a one-year-old lamb or goat. (If the family was small, they could combine with a neighboring family.) The most important detail was that the animal had to be perfect, one who was spotless and unblemished. God instructed them to slaughter the lamb, spread its blood over their doorposts and lintels, and roast the meat over fire. As instructed, they ate it with bitter herbs and unleavened bread. They didn't have time for bread to rise. God had instructed them to be dressed and ready to travel at a moment's notice. Their obedience to these instructions showed their faith and trust in Him, even if they were still in bondage.

Consider difficult events and situations in your life. When have you acted in faith, not knowing the outcome but trusting God even in the midst of uncertainty? How did your faith grow through these experiences?

That night, the lamb's blood on the doorposts set apart and protected the Israelites. However, the death of the firstborn impacted every home in Egypt.

Read Exodus 12:29-34.

In their fear, Pharaoh and the Egyptians immediately sent out the Israelites. Exodus 12:36 says, "And the LORD gave the people such favor with the Egyptians that they gave them what they requested. In this way they plundered the Egyptians." This verse reveals the fulfillment of Genesis 15:14. The Israelites were free and left Egypt with many possessions, just as God has promised Abraham.

What emotions do you think the Israelites experienced as they left Egypt? How are these emotions similar to times you have experienced God's provision or promises?

God called the Israelites to celebrate Passover annually as a reminder of the night that "He passed over the houses of the Israelites in Egypt when he struck the Egyptians, and he spared our homes" (Ex. 12:27). The blood of the lamb marked the Israelites as God's people and spared them from the death of the firstborn. The herbs symbolized the bitterness of slavery, while the unleavened bread signified the haste with which they left Egypt. Year after year, this meal served as a reminder of how God had delivered His people.

In the New Testament, Luke reveals that Jesus' family traveled to Jerusalem annually for Passover. One of the few stories in Scripture from Jesus' childhood happens during this event (Luke 2:41-50). Perhaps the most significant Passover observance occurred when Jesus celebrated it with His disciples the night before

His death. Over a thousand years after the first Passover, Jesus ate the same meal hours before He died on the cross, but He gave it a new meaning—the Lord's Supper (we'll cover that in another session).

You've probably heard the phrase, "Scripture can never mean what it never meant."[3] Long before the Israelite nation grew and became enslaved in Egypt, God had a plan to rescue them. The shed blood of the lamb at the first Passover served a specific purpose for the Israelites. But Passover foreshadowed something far greater. Just as God had a plan to free the Israelites from death and slavery, God also had a plan to free us.

While the lamb's blood saved the Israelites from physical death and led to their freedom from Egyptian oppression, Jesus' blood sacrificed on the cross saved us from spiritual death and the oppression of sin. He died in our place, taking on Himself the punishment that we deserve and giving us freedom from sin and death. As 1 Peter 1:18-19 says, "For you know that you were redeemed from your empty way of life inherited from your ancestors, not with perishable things like silver or gold, but with the precious blood of Christ, like that of an unblemished and spotless lamb."

From the moment sin entered the world, God had a plan to redeem us. We were not overlooked or forgotten. God did not leave us helpless and in bondage to sin. Instead, He sent us His Son. Jesus Christ is our Passover Lamb.

> Write a prayer of praise to God for providing Jesus as our Passover Lamb, securing our freedom from sin and spiritual death. Thank Him for the ways that even in the midst of uncertainty, we can trust in His plans and purposes because Jesus overcame sin and death in our place. If there are areas of your life in which you're struggling to rest in Jesus' sacrifice on the cross, ask God to deepen your faith and trust in Him.

THE SACRIFICIAL SYSTEM: WHY THE CROSS?

by Elizabeth Hyndman

The cross stands central in our Easter traditions and depictions. We see it on wall decorations, kids' coloring sheets, jewelry, and more. Similarly, we sing about and celebrate Jesus' blood shed on the cross. We talk about being washed in the blood. The cross has come to symbolize our entire faith, which perhaps is fitting. But have we softened the torture and execution device used to crucify Jesus Christ to a knickknack on our shelves? Has His blood just become a line in our songs?

Easter celebrates Jesus' resurrection, but before that, we must somberly reflect on His execution.

If you grew up in church or around church people, you may know the answer to the question, "Why did Jesus die?" He died to save us from our sins. That is true, from a motivational standpoint. But, in the words of so many small children, "Why?"

The other question, then, is, "Why did Jesus have to die?"

How would you answer that question? Why did Jesus have to die?

The answer starts in the Old Testament. After Adam and Eve disobeyed God, they hid from Him because of their nakedness and shame. As you read on the first day of this Bible study, their sin led to a separation between human beings and God. We could no longer enter into the same close relationship with our holy God that Adam and Eve had in the garden.

Read Genesis 3:21.

What did God do for Adam and Eve?

This verse describes the first sacrifice in the Bible. Later on, God instituted a full sacrificial system through the law He gave to Moses.

Without looking it up, how would you define the word *sacrifice*?

There are a few definitions in the dictionary, but all involve giving something up. A sacrifice can be made as an act of worship, but in the biblical sense, sacrifices were typically offered both to worship and to gain something else, like forgiveness.

In the Bible, the Book of Leviticus outlines several types of sacrifices for the sake of God's people. Burnt offerings (Lev. 1; 6) signified appeasement for sin and complete devotion to God. Grain offerings (Lev. 2; 6) conveyed thanksgiving for the harvest. Fellowship offerings (Lev. 3,7,22,27) symbolized general thankfulness to God. Sin offerings (Lev. 2–5; 6; 12) were mandatory offerings made by the one who had sinned unintentionally or was unclean. Guilt offerings (Lev. 5–7; 14) were also mandatory for a person who had deprived another of his or her rights or who had desecrated something holy.

The guilt offering required a ram or a lamb without blemish to be killed. It required blood to be shed.

Read Leviticus 17:11 and Hebrews 9:22.

Why was blood required for the sacrifice?

Look up the word *atonement* online or in a dictionary. Write the definition in your own words below.

As image bearers of God, we desecrate the holy when we sin against God. When we disobey Him, we are creating a barrier between our perfect, holy, righteous Creator and ourselves. Atonement provides a restoration of that relationship.

For the Jews, God mandated a Day of Atonement that would take place once a year. On this day, an offering would be given for the sins of the people. The specific procedure for this day is outlined in Leviticus 16.

Read Leviticus 16.

List a few steps of the process the high priest went through in order to perform the sacrifice.

What does this process reveal about God?

The procedure for atonement through the Law was complicated, to say the least. The high priest performed this ritual once a year, making sure to get every step correct. God provided a way for His people to experience atonement for their sins, even as they were wandering in the desert, even as they were setting up kingdoms, even as God seemed silent. He provided a way for them to be with Him in fellowship.

Life is in the blood of both animals and humans, according to Scripture. Since we need atonement for our lives (Rom. 6:23), life must be sacrificed. Life for life.

Read Hebrews 10:1-18.

What was the problem with the old sacrificial system?

What sacrifice did Jesus offer "for sins forever"?

The old system provided a way for God to be with His people, but Jesus is a better Way. Because of His sacrifice, we do not have to perform cumbersome rituals every year and every time we sin. We do not have to be cleansed over and over again. We can trust what Jesus said from the cross—"It is finished" (John 19:30). A better sacrifice has been made.

Through Jesus' death on the cross we find salvation—a restored relationship with God and sanctification, or growth toward godliness. The sacrifice of the perfect, unblemished Lamb of God provided atonement once and forever.

Read Revelation 5:8-10.

Why is the Lamb worthy to open the scroll?

What does it mean that Jesus "purchased" or "redeemed" us?

How does this passage lead you to worship God? Try writing out a prayer or a praise to God for Jesus' sacrifice on the cross.

The cross and the blood of Christ stand central to the Easter story and our faith in all their gore, because we know these ugly pictures of death mean life to us. The cross and the blood represent the most beautiful thing to ever happen in the whole history of the world and to us.

Jesus shed His blood and died on a cross because we needed a life for ours. We needed atonement, redemption, and righteousness. We needed a sacrifice. Praise God for the perfect Lamb sent to be that sacrifice for us!

THE SUFFERING SERVANT FORETOLD IN PROPHECY

by Ashley Marivittori Gorman

Have you ever felt totally unprepared for something? Or been oblivious to a really important situation, wishing someone would have given you a heads-up about it? How could the situation have turned out differently with a heads-up?

In the Book of Isaiah, four "Servant Songs" appear, prophesying about a certain "servant" of the Lord (Isa. 42:1-9; 49:1-13; 50:4-9; and 52:13–53:12). Most of the Servant Songs depict this person as a better source of salvation than the idols of the nations. He would be a strong savior who establishes justice, restores fortunes, and rules benevolently over many who will bow to him.

In many ways, God's people were supposed to be this servant—a nation that would be pure and just instead of corrupt, be economically sound, prosperous, generous, and faithfully display the One true God to all the other nations, inviting them to worship Him and enjoy His benevolent rule over their lives and land.

But God's people failed in this calling. Instead of serving God and others, they served themselves. Instead of being pure and just, they were notoriously compromised, greedy, apathetic, and corrupt. Instead of being a light to the world, they were lost in a darkness of their own making. They simply could not fill the shoes of this servant, and it quickly became clear that another servant—a better and truer one—would have to fit the bill.

Why do you think God's people failed to be the servant to God and others they were supposed to be?

How have you failed to serve God and others the way you should?

While the first three Servant Songs prophesy of a strong savior and ruler, the final Servant Song sings a strikingly different tune, as it paints a painful picture of the servant's great suffering.

> Read Isaiah 53 and describe what you discover about the Suffering Servant. List things such as what He would look like, what He would suffer, and what He would accomplish.

Throughout the various periods of Israel's history, it was no surprise to God's people for the Lord to raise up various leaders to deliver them in moments of trouble. Also, their Law, oral history, and songs had whispers of a chosen leader who would one day come to permanently take the throne of David. They were ready for a deliverer to free them, for an eternal king who would rule them benevolently forever. God had promised this in many ways and at many times. So the three other Servant Songs would have fit quite nicely into their expectations.

But a sufferer? A despised, feeble, unimpressive reject of society? That would hardly seem fitting when they had been promised such a strong, permanent ruler to come from their God.

Can you imagine the puzzled looks when the Suffering Servant prophecy made its way around town? *Wait, Isaiah, why all the suffering?*

This chosen servant is not painted as a great and mighty warrior, deliverer, king, or anyone else God's people might expect. Instead, the language Isaiah uses screams of the sacrificial system. Isaiah's point is clear: this Suffering Servant is not primarily interested in saving the people from their circumstantial enemies or troubles (though He cares for those things). He is out to save them from something far worse, far broader, and far more pervasive: sin.

As it turns out, God's people (and us, too!) were misguided in what they truly needed deliverance from. They didn't need to be saved from the things going on around them, they needed to be saved from themselves.

But why? Ever since the fall, sin had spread across the world like wildfire, wreaking havoc in every human heart and every human action. It spilled out everywhere, including God's people, creating an impenetrable barrier between humankind and God. It was the very thing creating all the other woes the people faced. So instead of dealing with their immediate dilemmas—whether that be relational or political or financial or physical—the Suffering Servant deals with the human dilemma. And He does so in a specific way.

As we learned last week, the only way to remove sin is through sacrifice. And since sin is the real enemy, we don't see the Suffering Servant getting up on a white horse to fight this battle. We see Him get down on an altar. He knows a perfect substitute is required to pay for His people's sin, and He pays it Himself, with His own blood.

Yes, the Servant has great plans for the people. Yes, He will take them into freedom and fairness and fortune one day. Those prophecies about the Servant are true, too! But before He takes them anywhere, He must first take their place.

What is the relationship between the human dilemma of sin and all the other dilemmas we face in life?

In what situations of your life are you asking Jesus to come deal with your circumstances instead of dealing with your sin?

In Isaiah's day, the people of God looked forward to when the Suffering Servant would come. In our day, we look back knowing He has already come. While there are numerous prophecies from the Old Testament fulfilled during Jesus' Passion Week, let's take some time to explore the ones specifically outlined in Isaiah 53.

VERSES	WHAT PROPHECY WAS FULFILLED?
Isa. 53:1 vs. John 12:37-38	
Isa. 53:2 vs. Phil. 2:6-8	
Isa. 53:3 vs. Luke 4:28-29	

Isa. 53:4 vs. Matt. 8:16-17	
Isa. 53:5 vs. Rom. 5:1; 2 Cor. 5:21	
Isa. 53:6 vs. 1 John 4:10	
Isa. 53:7 vs. Matt. 27:12-14	
Isa. 53:8 vs. John 18:13-22	
Isa. 53:9 vs. Matt. 27:57-60	
Isa. 53:10 vs. Luke 24:26; Heb. 2:10	
Isa. 53:11 vs. Rom. 5:8-9	
Isa. 53:12a vs. Luke 23:32-43	

The Suffering Servant chapter is a very intense prophecy. So, why would God inspire Isaiah to even include something so gruesome? Because God wanted His people to rightly recognize the Servant when He finally came on the scene, else they'd probably miss Him as their heads looked left and right for someone flashier. With this prophecy, God was being intentional to prepare His people, giving them a heads-up to look out for someone unexpected, someone who took the form of a *sacrifice* before He took on the form of a ruler. God wanted His people to know that this Servant had been in the plan for a long, long time, and they needed to be ready to spot Him when it was time.

And God wants us to know the very same things. Because of this prophecy, we can easily look back and identify Jesus as this Servant, and instead of seeing His death as a random or cruel historical accident, we can now see it for exactly what it is: part of God's intentional plan to save us all.

LONGING FOR A KING

by Savannah Ward

I have always been a planner. From the time I was a little girl, I had a clipboard, sticky notes, and a plan. From my strategy to obtain a desired pet, to long-term life goals, I believed that I knew best and made every effort to see my plans come to fruition.

At a young age, I mapped out my plan for my life: get married right out of college, become a famous Broadway actress, have kids, and live happily ever after. Today, I am in my late twenties, serving behind the scenes rather than center stage, and engaged to marry a wonderful man, but not before we endured the heartache of a three-year break up after our college relationship.

It is safe to say that my life today is certainly not the life I envisioned when I was ten years old. There has been pain and disappointment—often self-inflicted. Yet, thankfully, the God who knows better than me had a plan.

Have you ever thought you knew what was best in a situation only to find that someone wiser than you knew better?

In the Bible, the Israelites experienced a similar desire to construct their own plan. Samuel, who served as a judge of Israel, was appointed by God to deliver and save Israel from her enemies. As Samuel grew old, he appointed his sons as judges of Israel to take his place after his death. However, his sons did not share Samuel's godly character and nobility, and because of their sin, the elders of Israel felt the two men were unfit to lead. So the elders formulated a solution for their perceived leadership dilemma—a king. When the people told Samuel they wanted him to appoint a king as leader, he was troubled by this request and asked God for direction.

Read 1 Samuel 8:7-9.

How did God respond to Samuel's prayer?

As God instructed, Samuel granted the people's desire for a king, but not without warning. Samuel described the role of the king and the inevitable cost to the people. Still, they wanted a king to judge them and go before them and fight their battles (v. 20).

For the next forty-two generations, the kingdoms of Israel and Judah were ruled by kings—some godly leaders, but many were evil. Just as Samuel warned the people, the kings took for themselves from the people and did what they pleased rather than seeking God. Even the godliest kings fell short and left the people lacking the leader they desired.

Like the Israelites, we often think we know best. We want to do things ourselves and often attempt to formulate solutions to solve our problems. And again, like the Israelites, we too are left empty when we trust ourselves rather than God.

But in His wisdom and grace, God gave His people the desires of their hearts. He knew that Israel longed for a king, a true King. Not for an earthly king who, no matter how godly, would inevitably fall short in character and ability to save the people from their enemies and death. God knew that the desire He placed in their hearts for a king was one that He alone could satisfy.

As the people waited and groaned for a better king, one who would finally conquer and fulfill their longing, God revealed through the prophet Isaiah that He would send the ultimate King (Isa. 7:14). Centuries later, an angel appeared to a virgin, telling her she would give birth to a Son and that He was the One of whom Isaiah spoke.

Read Luke 1:32-33 and write it below.

After forty-two generations of earthly kings, the ultimate King came to Israel in the most unexpected way. Jesus came and lived among His people. He was not the earthy king they expected, but an eternal King who changed everything.

Toward the end of His earthly ministry, Jesus revealed to His disciples how He was the fulfillment of the people's longings.

Read John 16:33 and write what Jesus declared in this passage.

Jesus was the King longed for by the people in 1 Samuel 8—a just and conquering King who went before them to fight their battles (v. 20).

Although the people of Israel chose to trust their own plans more than they trusted God, God allowed their brokenness and longing to display their true need. God looked beyond the needs of their spoken desires to the needs of their hearts— needs that He alone could fulfill. Through Jesus, not only did God fulfill their true desire for a King, He also redeemed their brokenness and efforts to make things right for themselves with the King who came to make all things right.

So often, like the Israelites, we trust ourselves more than we trust God. We believe we know best for our lives and attempt to accomplish victory through our own efforts. Yet God, rich in mercy, sent us a King to save us. Not an earthly king who takes, but Jesus, the ultimate King, who gives—even His own life for us.

This humble King, born of the lineage of David, came to conquer death, go before us, and fight the battle we could not. Just days before that victory, He made His triumphant entry into Jerusalem, the city of kings, before an anticipating, longing Israel—and a captive, waiting world.

In what areas of your life do you trust your own judgment more than God's guidance?

Is Jesus the victorious King of your life today? If not, why not?

Pray, confessing your sin of being your own king and ask Christ to take His rightful place as King of your heart and life.

make a

Confessional
Wreath

by Larissa Arnault Roach

Set the tone for the Easter season by embracing the practice of confession. Confession of sin to God brings forgiveness and restores our fellowship with Him (Ps. 32; 51; 1 John 1:9). Confessing to each other is a vulnerable activity that provides support, accountability, and restoration within the body of Christ (Gal. 6:1-2; Jas. 5:16).

You may have participated in a stations of the cross service prior to Easter Sunday where you physically drove nails into a wooden cross. Then on Easter, the holes left from the nails were filled with flowers as a celebrative display. The following activity is a simple way to personalize that celebration at home.

GATHER

- Styrofoam wreath or grapevine
- Toothpicks
- Fresh flowers (for Easter Sunday)

DIRECTIONS

Place a styrofoam wreath and cup of toothpicks on the center of your table a month before Easter. (If you are feeling extra festive, you can spray paint the wreath or wrap it with thin ribbon.) Whether yours is a table for one or if it seats many, each evening when you sit down to dinner, practice confessing your sin out loud and insert a toothpick into the wreath with each admission. While this practice might be uncomfortable at first (indeed, it is difficult to examine our hearts), the physical and verbal act is profound. Hopefully over time you will become more aware of your sin and see patterns that need to change. The most wonderful news is that this activity does not end with confession! On Easter morning before others in your home wake up, replace the toothpick indentions with beautiful spring flowers. This reminds us that His mercies are new every morning, and Christ came to forgive our sin.

share your story of

Redemption

by Amanda Mejias

How tragic would it have been for the redemption story to have ended with Genesis 3? Can you imagine if God said to Adam and Eve, "Well, good luck figuring your way out of this one!" But we know their story wasn't over. God's plan was just beginning and redemption was coming.

You have probably heard the words "My life is over" come out of your teen's mouth at some point. Those words seem dramatic, but don't you remember life in middle and high school? A failing grade or broken relationship truly felt like the end of the world. Even the smallest things felt so big. And you know what feels really big as a teenager? Sin.

It's common for teens to get caught up with sins like lying, cheating, viewing pornography, and so on. But most teens aren't ignorant to the seriousness of these sins and why they shouldn't be engaging in those behaviors. However, if they are never given hope for redemption and restoration, they will feel hopeless to move forward and locked into that sinful struggle.

We may understand there is no sin too great for God to forgive and no past too dirty for Him to make clean, but does your teen know this? Does he truly know what redemption could look like for him? One of the best ways your teen is going to learn about redemption is through your example.

Set aside some time this week to talk to your teen about your redemption story. Share your story of coming to Christ. Be honest about your need for Jesus and how He has freed you from past struggles with sin. If you don't feel comfortable sharing everything in a face-to-face conversation, you could write it out in a letter to him. After he reads it, you could discuss it together. Either way, encourage your teen to always come to you if he has questions about salvation or about how to find freedom from sins. As one final activity for this week, memorize this verse with your teen:

> Once you were alienated
> and hostile in your minds as
> expressed in your evil actions.
> But now he has reconciled you
> by his physical body through
> his death, to present you
> holy, faultless, and blameless
> before him.
>
> COLOSSIANS 1:21-22

make an
Easter Garland

by Kayla Stevens

The whole Bible is about Jesus. It is the story of God's plan to send Jesus to rescue us from sin. All of the Old Testament points forward to Jesus' life, death, and resurrection. As we look forward to celebrating Easter, we remember the hope we have in Jesus.

GATHER

- plastic eggs
- slips of paper
- an empty jar
- white kitchen twine

Gather your supplies and work with your family to make Easter garland. Each day your family will add truths about Jesus to the Easter garland in anticipation of Easter.

Puncture a hole in each end of the egg. Insert the twine into one end of the plastic egg and string it through the other end. Tie a small knot at each end of each egg to hold it in place. Be sure to leave a small amount of space to open and close each plastic egg.

Then, a few weeks before Easter, collect several slips of paper and place them in an empty jar. Encourage your family to think about truths you know about Jesus from the Old and New Testaments. Include truths you learn throughout this study. Write down one truth on a different slip of paper each day leading up to Easter and place it in one of the plastic eggs on your Easter garland. With older children, consider writing down Bible verses that match each truth. For example: Jesus is the promised Messiah—Isaiah 9:6; God sent Jesus to earth with a purpose—John 3:16. Briefly discuss each truth or verse as you place it in an egg.

On Easter Sunday, open all of the plastic eggs as a family and celebrate Jesus' resurrection.

Passion Week Begins

WEEK 2

With the Contrite and Lowly

by Sarah Doss

The Old Testament saints yearned for rescue over many centuries, looking in hope toward the coming Messiah. Yet many of the faithful Hebrew followers of God had trouble believing that Jesus was the Rescuer who had been foretold. What's the deal? Why was it so hard for the first-century world, especially God's chosen people, to believe that Jesus was the answer to the prayer their community of faith had collectively prayed over the years?

Though Jesus was and is perfectly God, He seemed a bundle of contradictions for the people of Israel. During Jesus' time, the Jews were living under Roman rule and had been for several years. They were looking for God's kingdom to come and many thought God would send a savior as a powerful political and military leader who would stand up for them and vanquish their enemies.

As we'll see this week, though Jesus was powerful and impressive in many ways—He most often walked a humble path, one that frustrated and threatened the religious leaders of His day. Jesus was always faithful to God's will and God's ways. But the way Jesus followed God ran counter to many of the rules and principles the leaders espoused. In His merciful, lowly way, Jesus sought out the downtrodden, the contrite. He showed the people that their concept of God, His kingdom, and His Law was a bit askew. And in teaching God's Word, healing the sick, and leading the disciples—among other things—we see Jesus breaking down many of the man-made barriers that (unbeknownst to us) kept us away from God.

He showed them (and shows us) the lies we've believed about God and replaces those lies with brilliant truths, full of patient, pursuing grace. He shows us the kindness of our heavenly Father. He shows us the justice and righteousness of a holy God. He used the seemingly simple things around Him to illustrate critical and comforting truths—how lilies and sparrows show us we can trust God for provision without worrying (Matt. 6:26) and how the mountains remind us of God's steadfast and unshakable love for us (Isa. 54:10). And He shows us how to prioritize—how the object of our faith, God, is most important; how the state of our hearts before God and others is highly valued, above our attempts to please Him by looking or acting a certain way.

Jesus, Emmanuel, God with us—brought freedom from the brokenness of this world that weighed us down and shed light on the beauty of God to come. Considering Jesus brings to mind Isaiah 57:15 (ESV):

> For thus says the One who is high and lifted up,
>
> who inhabits eternity, whose name is Holy:
>
> "I dwell in the high and holy place,
>
> and also with him who is of a contrite and lowly spirit,
>
> to revive the spirit of the lowly,
>
> and to revive the heart of the contrite."

Jesus showed us what it looked like for God to both be high and holy and yet to stoop and see our need. Jesus sought out the contrite; He told His children to "take heart" despite the difficulties. Over and over again, He revived the spirits of the lowly.

You'll likely notice that people had some pretty contradictory reactions to Jesus. As you're reading this week, pay attention to Jesus' heart—His steady obedience to God and purposeful care for His followers, no matter the circumstance.

This same Jesus who was praised on Palm Sunday and lowered Himself to serve His disciples sees you. He loves you. Won't you let Him revive your heart?

What was your favorite day of study this past week?

How do you see the kindness and love of God in the story of the fall? When you consider that God had a plan all along to bring us to redemption, what does that say about His character?

How is Jesus foreshadowed in the Passover story? Where are some other places we see the coming of Jesus foreshadowed in the Old Testament? Why is it important we understand all of Scripture points to Jesus?

Why did Jesus have to die? What was wrong with the old sacrificial system?

What does it mean for Jesus to be King of your life? Is this currently the case? If so, what is the evidence? If not, what keeps you from letting Him have full reign?

Close your time with prayer, taking a moment to assess who's truly in control of your life. Confess your desire to be in charge and surrender to Christ's lordship in your life. Commit to living wholeheartedly for Him this week.

A TRIUMPHANT ENTRY

by Ellen Vest

Growing up, it was a family tradition to gather around the television every Thanksgiving and watch the Macy's Thanksgiving Day Parade. We got up early, found the right channel, and settled in to be entertained by the balloons, the floats, and the singers.

It's still a tradition I observe with my own family. I tune in to the parade early, eager to point out all the character balloons to my daughter. I'll ask her if she saw this one or that one go by. She giggles at the sight of big balloons moving down the street. It's a morning of celebration and excitement for everyone.

When I think about the historical tradition of a conquering king returning triumphantly from battle riding a horse, I wonder if the people observing the victory march experienced similar emotions to those we feel watching this parade every year. But what if a man decided to ride a donkey to Manhattan's Herald Square on Thanksgiving Day? What questions would we be asking ourselves? Probably, things like: Who let this guy in? Why are people clapping for this? Is he lost?

Passion Week began with Palm Sunday, a day where the people of Jerusalem gathered at the gate to acclaim and celebrate. But it also began a week of confusing events. We have to remember the people at this time in history didn't know anything about Easter. They were days away from attending a very different kind of gathering. A gathering that would display a sacrifice for all of our sins.

This is the beginning of the last week of Jesus' life. On Palm Sunday, Jesus entered Jerusalem as a king. Of course, we will later see, it was not how a king in those times would ever dream of entering the city. Usually the conquering king entered on a mighty stallion. Jesus rode in humbly on a donkey.

I have always wanted to know what it was like to stand among the people that day, watching a man on a donkey enter the streets as if he were a triumphant king. What would I have whispered to my neighbor next to me? It would have been unlike anything I would have ever encountered before. I have always been curious about the buzz of the crowd that day. Perhaps not everyone was excited. There had to be people there—still filled with doubt. Surely Jesus knew there were some who weakly shouted "Hosanna!" who would later fervently shout "Crucify!" Even so, He still entered the city in victorious fashion.

Reread Matthew 21:1-11.

What were Jesus' instructions in verses 1-3?

Jesus instructed two disciples to go into the village and find a donkey and its foal tied up. They were to untie them and to tell anyone who had questions to simply say "the Lord needs them."

Take a quick look at Mark's version of this story in Mark 11:1-6.

What did the disciples encounter and how did they respond?

What does this interaction teach us about the obedience of the two disciples?

Read Isaiah 62:11 and Zechariah 9:9 and summarize the passages.

These Old Testament passages show how the Palm Sunday events had already been prophesied and took place so that the prophecy might be fulfilled.

That being said, how does this show us the importance of the way the events unfolded that day?

For Jesus to so perfectly fulfill this prophecy was a confirmation that He was the Messiah. The psalmist in Psalm 118:24-26 also referred to this specific day when he wrote:

> This is the day the LORD has made; let us rejoice and be glad in it. LORD, save us! LORD, please grant us success! He who comes in the name of the LORD is blessed. From the house of the LORD we bless you.

When they brought the donkey to Jesus, the disciples laid their own clothes on it for Jesus to sit on. Then, as Jesus moved into the city, the people spread their clothes on the road and branches from the trees as well. Now, let's pause for a minute here. We have a bunch of people who just realized they are in the presence of Jesus and He needs an entrance. I think the planner/organizer in me twitches a little bit at the thought of being caught in the middle of something so important and then just using my own clothes as the means to make an entrance for Jesus. You wouldn't pin that idea of laying clothes on the ground to your Pinterest board, now would you? Even so, this expression shows the humbleness of Jesus and His followers. Remember: This is the way it was always supposed to happen.

In Matthew 21:9, we read the crowd was shouting:

> Hosanna to the Son of David!
>
> Blessed is he who comes in the name of the Lord!
>
> Hosanna in the highest heaven!

Underline the words *Hosanna* and *blessed* in the verse above.

Hosanna is used to express adoration. It is a joyful Aramaic exclamation of praise for deliverance granted or anticipated. It is primarily used in the Gospels of Matthew and Mark to announce Jesus coming into Jerusalem. What a sweet word we have to use solely to exclaim our praise and anticipation of the Lord!

How do you uniquely praise and worship the Lord in your everyday life?

How does seeing Jesus' followers shout "Hosanna," even though they may not have realized what the rest of the week would hold, encourage you as you worship the Lord even when it isn't easy?

Review Matthew 21:10-11.

How did the city react when Jesus entered Jerusalem and how did the crowd describe Him? How did their description fall short?

The crowds announced Jesus as a prophet from Nazareth. Sure, it was a high honor, yet in coming days they would find Him to be so much more than that.

Do you ever sell short the power and presence of Christ in your life? Explain.

As you participate in the celebration of Palm Sunday and the beginning of Holy Week, I urge you to picture yourself in the crowd that day. Are you joyfully exclaiming "Hosanna! Hosanna!"? Do you truly see and understand Jesus to be the King of kings and Lord of lords in your life, or is He something less than that? Maybe you're taking a minute to absorb everything going on and wondering who this Jesus really is.

In this Easter season, I urge us all to pause and pray and reflect on who Jesus really is and what kind of followers of Christ we are.

JESUS' TEACHING

by Susan Hill

The writer, Annie Dillard, said, "How we spend our days is, of course, how we spend our lives."[1] We live in an era where there are countless ways to spend, invest, or waste time. If we aren't careful, there's a good chance we'll fail to get the most out of our days. The Bible isn't silent about time management and has much to say about living with intentionality. Jesus was the Master Teacher, and He modeled what it looked like to live with laser-like focus.

As Calvary loomed, Jesus knew the time He had left with His disciples was limited. They'd given up everything to follow Him, and for three years, they'd walked shoulder to shoulder with Jesus, learning what it meant to be His disciples. Still, they were unsure about what was coming. Jesus knew their world was going to be shattered, and He wanted to prepare them for not only what was coming but how to live prepared after He was gone. So on the brink of Jesus' departure, He taught His disciples how to be ready for His return.

During the last days of His earthly ministry, Jesus reflected on how He'd spent His time on earth. In the High Priestly Prayer, Jesus prayed to the Father, saying: "I have glorified you on the earth by completing the work you gave me to do" (John 17:4). As Jesus retraced His steps, He could say with confidence He'd been obedient to the Father and completed the work He'd been given to do.

Eventually, all of us will face a similar scenario. Our time in this world will come to an end. It will either arrive by way of death or Christ's second coming—whichever comes first. At that point, it will be too late to rethink our priorities. How we live during this life has ramifications that will impact us for eternity, so it's crucial we're mindful of that reality. Jesus knew this was the case, and so it was a topic He taught on during the last week of His ministry. In Matthew 25, we find teaching that speaks to living with intentionality and being prepared for Christ's return. It's a message that's just as relevant today as when Jesus taught it to His disciples during Passion Week.

Read Matthew 25:1-13.

What is the lesson in this parable and how does it apply to your life?

Are you living prepared for Jesus' coming? If so, what's the evidence? If not, what needs to change?

Jesus told the story of ten virgins, who are similar to bridesmaids in a wedding, awaiting the arrival of the groom. Five of the women came prepared with enough oil in their lamps, but the other five were caught off guard and unprepared. As a result, the latter group was denied entrance into the wedding banquet (v. 12). It's obvious then, that the kingdom of God is not for those who merely respond to an invitation. All ten of the bridesmaids had responded to the invitation, but five of them didn't persevere. In the same way, we often see people respond to an invitation to follow Jesus, but after time passes, they fall away. Maybe at some point they even felt genuine affection for Christ, but they were never truly His. They lacked the faith to stay the course. The Bible teaches that saving faith perseveres to the end (Matt. 24:12-13; Mark 4:16-19; Heb. 3:14).

Read Matthew 25:14-30.

What's the message here for how we are to live as followers of Christ?

In the parable of the talents, Jesus spoke of three servants who were entrusted with specific talents from their master. During the master's absence, one of the servants invested his five talents and earned five more. Likewise, the man possessing two talents invested his talents and earned two more. But the third man found no joy in serving his master and thought him to be difficult, so he buried his only talent and got nothing in return. Because of the third man's lack of faith, and unwillingness to maximize what he'd been entrusted, the master took the servant's only talent and gave it to the man who had ten talents (v. 28).

A close look at the text reveals the third man's attitude toward his master impacted how he stewarded his resources. He had no love or reverence for his master, and so he was lazy with the resources his master entrusted to him. To be sure, our salvation is by grace through faith, and it can't be earned by works (Eph. 2:8-9). However, if our faith is genuine, we will be good stewards of what God has entrusted to us as an expression of our love for Him. This parable begs the question: do we want to be people who live with intentionality motivated by our love for God, or be people who are condemned for our laziness?

How are you using the gifts, talents, and skills God has given you to honor Him and move His kingdom forward?

Read Matthew 25:31-46.

The first two stories were parables. Do you think this teaching is also a parable, or is it something different? Explain.

While this teaching may sound like parable, it is more a glimpse of what's to come in the final judgment. It's a real event that will take place in the future.[2]

How would you summarize this teaching?

Jesus describes a time when all people will stand before Him. The sheep—God's people—will be on His right. The goats—who represent the lost—will be on the left (v. 33). The Son of Man will commend those on His right for providing food, water, shelter, clothing, hospitality, and medical care for the "least of these." It's notable that in this context, Jesus was referring to believers who came to the aid of their brothers and sisters in Christ (Matt. 25:40). That's not to say Christians aren't called to help nonbelievers—many places in the Bible speak to helping all people—but in this instance, Jesus is speaking of helping other Christians. Again, these gracious acts are not a means of salvation, but they are evidence of a heart that has been changed by God.

In this parable, the believers whom Jesus commended for their acts of mercy were surprised and even asked, "Lord, when did we see you hungry and feed you, or thirsty and give you something to drink?" (v. 37). It's clear that their motive in serving those in need was not an attempt at earning righteousness but was a result of their love for God and other people. Scripture shows that our love for other believers is a mark of an authentic Christian (John 15:12).

> If Jesus were to come today, how do you think He would assess your love and care for the least of these?

Jesus is our Master, and He has given us everything we need for life and godliness (2 Pet. 1:3). It would be insulting to the cross of Christ to believe we could pay Him back. But if we love Him, we will be mindful of a time coming when we will see Him face-to-face and give an account for how we have lived (2 Cor. 5:10). It's vital that we work diligently to maximize the gifts and resources He has given us during our time on this earth. If our faith doesn't change the way we live, there's good reason to question its authenticity (Jas. 2:14). Genuine faith will motivate us to live a life that brings glory to God and anticipate the day we will see His face.

DECISIONS, DECISIONS

by Rachel Shaver

One of my sons struggles with decision-making. When he has a choice to make, even a choice between two seemingly good things like milk chocolate or dark chocolate, he agonizes over what to do. (As if there's really any comparison ... Ahem.) His question to me or his dad is always, "But which one *is better*?"

This is the very question that brought sin into the world: *which choice do I think will be better for me?* In Adam and Eve's case, they were deceived into believing that God's way wasn't best for them. So, they chose to disobey—they chose sin. And that one, seemingly small decision to take a bite of forbidden fruit? It changed everything.

Read Mark 14:3-9. Then read John 12:3.

Jesus was having dinner with friends. While He was there, a woman came to him with an alabaster flask full of pure nard. (Because nard isn't a word we throw around a lot in dinner conversations nowadays, I'll break it down for you: rare, expensive perfume. You're welcome.)

This woman in Mark's account is identified in John's Gospel as Mary—the same Mary who chose to sit at Jesus' feet and listen to His teachings instead of being distracted by less important work like her sister Martha (Luke 10:38-42). Also, something to note: Mary and Martha were the sisters of Lazarus, the man whom Jesus raised from the dead. To put it bluntly, Mary didn't just know about Jesus, *she knew Jesus.* And she knew He was worthy of all she had to offer.

How much does Mark 14:5 say that the nard was worth?

That's right—three hundred denarii. In the first century, three hundred denarii would have been almost equivalent to a year's salary! To say that her action was significant would be an understatement. Scripture tells us something interesting about her action—she broke the alabaster flask of nard to pour over Jesus' head. She wanted every last drop of that precious perfume for Jesus because she knew He was worth it. Her decision didn't come without criticism though.

What does Mark 9:4-5 tell us about how others reacted to her decision and why they reacted that way?

Ridiculed. John 12:5 tells us that she was especially ridiculed by a man named Judas. We will talk more about him in a minute. According to Judas, there was a better use for Mary's jar of nard than Jesus.

What lie does this remind you of?

Right, again—the original lie that Satan told Eve in the garden. Satan told her he knew a better use for the forbidden fruit and a better way than what God offered. The truth is, Jesus didn't need that jar of nard to be poured out for Him. He doesn't need anything from us at all. This was an act of worship on the part of Mary. She knew who was most precious. So while her decision might not have made sense to the world around her, she made it anyway—as a way to show her love and declare who her Savior was.

Have you ever chosen to do something that you knew God was calling you to do, even though you knew it might not make sense to the people in your life? Write about that decision here.

Our decisions to be obedient to Christ might not make much sense to our friends and family. It might mean picking up and moving across the world or declining the dream job. It might be breaking off a special relationship or telling our kids "no," when every other parent is saying, "yes." Our decision to follow Jesus will likely require sacrifice in the way of time, money, relationships, being ridiculed, or other things, but we, like Mary, must remember that Jesus is worthy.

Read John 13:21-30.

Again, we see Jesus with a group of people—His disciples. We read in this passage that Judas, one of Jesus' twelve disciples, would betray Him. Now, as Jesus' disciple, Judas would have been in very close physical proximity to Jesus—as Jesus performed miracles, as He taught, as He lived everyday life as a man on this earth. So, Judas knew who Jesus was, but did he know Jesus like Mary knew Him? If anyone could have believed that Jesus was the Son of God and worthy, no matter the cost, then surely it would have been His disciples, right?

Read Mark 14:10-11 out loud.

What does Scripture tell us Judas traded Jesus for?

Money. Judas betrayed Jesus for money. It sounds absolutely ridiculous when we read it out loud, doesn't it? Judas fell prey to Satan, the father of deception, with a different version of the same lie: *Jesus isn't enough for you.*

What lies have you believed about what might be better than following Jesus?

Ouch. I know it hurts to write it down. I know I have a long, long list of things that I have chosen over Jesus. But just like Jesus knew that Judas was going to betray Him (John 13:21), He knew I would choose to believe the lie that God was holding His goodness back from me too.

Jesus is sovereign! He knew what He was facing by dying on the cross—a cross that He didn't have to die on, but chose to die on. And why? Because of His never-ending, unmatched love for us.

What beauty lies in Jesus' decision to follow the will of His Father! Because of His choice to die for us, we are forgiven for all of the times that we trade Jesus for what we think is better. This is the good news of the cross. Instead of being a slave to our sinful decisions, we get freedom from them! Jesus chose death so that we could be free to live in the midst of God and His goodness for eternity.

SERVING THE DISCIPLES

by Connia Nelson

There is something uniquely different about someone who puts others before herself. She exudes loving-kindness and has a light that shines from within, making everything around her just a little bit brighter. My mother was that kind of person.

My mom's home was a place of comfort for all who entered. When you stepped inside her door, the sweet and savory aromas from her kitchen drew you in. She was an excellent cook and an even better baker. To this day, her friends and family still comment on how warm and welcoming it was to be in her presence and without fail they will mention her famous homemade dinner rolls. My mom was a godly woman who selflessly and sometimes sacrificially served her family and guests. Serving was never beneath her, instead it was a blessing and an honor. I learned valuable life lessons on how to lovingly care for others simply by watching her serve with humility and grace.

The disciples hung out with Jesus for three years. They watched Him heal the sick, raise the dead, feed thousands and often socialize with people whom others shunned. They were firsthand witnesses to His many acts of service throughout His ministry. And yet on their last evening with Him, they were not prepared for His gracious service to them. Jesus knew His time had come and soon He would die on the cross for the sins of the world.

Read John 13:1-16.

Most of us have seen the painting by Leonardo da Vinci depicting Jesus and the disciples sitting behind a banquet table. However, the table arrangement is not culturally accurate. In his book, *The Forgotten Jesus*, Robby Gallaty, points out how first-century Jews would have reclined on cushions lying on their sides next to a low U-shaped table. The middle section of the table was open for serving food and entertainment. Guests reclined with their legs extending away from the table allowing servants access to wash their feet during the meal.[3]

The disciples were stunned when Jesus stood, wrapped a towel around His waist, poured water in a basin, knelt, and began washing their feet. This action was outrageous. Surely the King of kings and Lord of lords should not be doing this lowly act. The job of washing feet in those days was given to the lowest of servants, a slave actually, and yet our Lord displayed humble servant leadership in this moment.

What does John 13:1 say about how Jesus loved His disciples?

Jesus loved the disciples to the very end. He didn't just say He loved them, He showed them and proved to them He did not come to be served but to serve (Mark 10:45). He even washed the feet of the one who would betray Him that same night. What an amazing demonstration of love and complete humility.

Would you be able to humble yourself to serve an enemy? What would it take for you to be able to put self aside and serve?

When it was Peter's turn for his feet to be washed, he defiantly and disobediently objected, telling Jesus "You will never wash my feet." But when Jesus told Peter that refusing to have his feet washed meant he would have no part with Him, Peter quickly changed his tune and immediately asked the Lord to wash not only his feet but also his hands, and his head! Peter's heart was in the right place, but he was missing the point entirely. That's why Jesus explained that once you have been bathed, there's no need to take another bath, you just need to wash your dirty feet.

The assurance for believers is once you've been washed in the blood of the Lamb, you are saved and never need to be saved again. However, as long as you live on this earth, you'll continue to struggle with sin. There are going to be times when you mess up and need forgiveness for a particular sin in your life. The promise of 1 John 1:9 says:

> If we confess our sins, he is faithful and righteous to forgive us our sins and to cleanse us from all unrighteousness.

Isn't that just like God? Not only did He send His Son to save us, but He also provided a way for us to be forgiven when we go astray so we can stay clean!

I am always enamored with Jesus' teachable moments. In John 13:12, Jesus reclined at the table and asked the disciples, "Do you know what I have done for you?"

He wanted the disciples to understand that just as He had washed their feet, they should do the same for each other. They needed this lesson because Luke records that at this supper, the disciples had actually argued over who would be the greatest (Luke 22:24). Jesus emphasized that the servant is not greater than his master. He was teaching the disciples both the act of service and the very important lesson of having a servant's heart. A servant's heart goes beyond the act of service to having a servant's character that humbly serves and meets the needs of others for the glory of God. Where true humility exists, there is no room for arrogance and self-promotion. If you want to be great, serve others.

Rick Warren said, "This is true humility: not thinking less of ourselves but thinking of ourselves less."[4] Those who want to be great in God's eyes allow themselves to be less in the eyes of man. The best way to understand humble service is by example, and that's what Jesus provided in this passage. One of the greatest virtues to grow and develop in our personal, professional, and spiritual lives is a humble servant's heart. A true servant leader offers to perform tasks no one else will do, just as Jesus did when He washed the disciples' feet.

Consider the opportunities you have to humbly serve. What motivates and excites you to serve?

Do you have someone in your life who has a servant's heart? What can you learn by watching this person serve God and others?

On that night before His death, Jesus showed His disciples and us what greatness is all about—humbling onself, washing feet, being a servant. Let's follow His example.

THE LORD'S SUPPER

by Debbie Dickerson

A pressed flower, a well-loved baby's blanket, an old photo—we keep these things to recall a cherished time, to keep us connected with those we love, and to remind us to be thankful for the blessings as we face the coming days. When something changes the familiar in our lives to something new, remembering helps us look back and see God at work in those life-changing moments.

What keepsakes do you have? Is there one that especially reminds you of God's presence—His sovereign work and unfailing love? Explain.

Much like our life-changing moments, this biblical epoch began with the familiar: a celebration that had been part of Jewish history since the exodus from Egypt. But this imminent evening became unforgettable in the stretch of eternity. As the sun set, a tick mark on the timeline of past, present, and future hinged in history. The page turned past the 14th of Nisan on the Jewish calendar (from Thursday of Passion Week) as Jesus gathered with His twelve disciples in an upper room in Jerusalem for a meal made to remember.

Throughout the evening, Jesus unfolded God's sovereign plan of salvation, moving from the prophetic promise to the messianic fulfillment and on to the future assurance of the reunion of the family of God.

The tone had been set with Jesus' arrival in Jerusalem on a donkey, the King of kings fulfilling prophecy. Now with the table set, the disciples arrived, expecting the traditional Passover meal.

Recall what you learned about Passover (Week 1, Day 2). Then read Luke 22:14-15. How did Jesus feel about this time with His disciples? What was going to happen to Him?

In the original Greek language, Jesus' phrase "fervently desired" is emphatic, using repetition to show the passion behind His words: "I have desired with great desire." Although this wasn't the first time the disciples had been told of His suffering, Jesus' passion paired with the reminder should have raised the eyebrows of those around the table to notice the meal was changing course.

Read Matthew 26:26; Mark 14:22; and Luke 22:19.

What did Jesus do with the bread? In Luke's account, notice the pronoun "you" and replace it with your name.

"As they were eating …" leads us to the part of the Passover meal when the roasted lamb likely would have been served. Sitting among the disciples, Jesus represented the Passover lamb foreshadowed in Exodus 12. They watched as He took bread, gave thanks, broke it, and gave it to them. It would be understood that breaking bread together was an act of friendship and shared trust. But more so, years of taking this unleavened bread would have taught them the urgency of the exodus. Now Jesus would teach them the greater significance.

The disciples would have readily recognized Jesus' next words as out of the ordinary: "This is my body, which is given for you" (Luke 22:19). Seeing Jesus' unbroken body there before them, the disciples would have understood this as a Hebraic metaphor, not a miraculous changing of the bread to become His body literally or in any other way. Jesus gave the bread and said, "Do this in remembrance of me" (Luke 22:19; 1 Cor. 11:24)—a symbolic reminder of His pending sacrificial death for their sins.

But the disciples could not yet behold their King as the sacrificial Lamb. And if we read the words "given for you" too quickly, we'll miss the weight of redemption, the eternal plan promised at the fall of Adam and Eve and proclaimed throughout the ages. Passover as the disciples knew it had just changed forever.

Read Matthew 26:27-28; Mark 14:23-24; and Luke 22:20.

What did Jesus do next? Write in your own words what He said.

With the meal completed, Jesus took the third cup—the cup of blessing. But instead of this cup representing the blood of an animal sacrificed for sins to be passed over, Jesus said, "This cup is the new covenant in my blood" (Luke 22:20). With this statement, Jesus used the cup to symbolize the shedding of His blood "for the forgiveness of sins" (Matt. 26:28), "which is poured out for many" (Mark 14:24), "which is poured out for you" (Luke 22:20).

All have sinned, including you and me. And sin separates us from holy God who has deemed that "without the shedding of blood there is no forgiveness" (Heb. 9:22). To reconcile us to God, Jesus offered His blood as the final sacrifice, replacing the old covenant written in stone with the promised new covenant written on the hearts of His children. (See Jer. 31:31-34.)

This was Jesus' last supper with His disciples. But don't miss the most wonderful reunion He promises to the family of God.

Read Matthew 26:29; Mark 14:25; and Luke 22:18.

What was the promise and where will this take place (Rev. 19:6-9)?

After Jesus promised to continue the meal in the kingdom of God, He and the remaining eleven (Judas having been dismissed to fulfill his betrayal), sang a hymn, probably some of the Hallel (a portion of Ps. 113–118 that was recited during Passover meals. The name comes from the Hebrew for "Praise Thou.")[5] The phrase "His faithful love endures forever" (Ps. 118:29) is the heart behind that promised reunion.

Throughout the meal and on the way to the Mount of Olives, Jesus taught His disciples of His death and resurrection and the coming of the Holy Spirit. Then serving as the High Priest preparing to make the ultimate sacrifice of Himself, Jesus "looked up to heaven, and said, 'Father, the hour has come. Glorify your Son so that the Son may glorify you'" (John 17:1). Affirming His purpose in coming to earth, He continued the High Priestly Prayer, interceding for the disciples (John 17:1-19) and for us.

Read John 17:20-26.

What did Jesus pray for us in this passage?

Notice the intimacy He expressed in John 17:23—"I am in them and you are in me, so that they may be made completely one, that the world may know you have sent me and have loved them as you have loved me."

Jesus knew how easily we forget and how forgetting can cause us to stray in our relationship with God. So, on His last earthly night He served a meal intended to help us remember Him and prayed for us.

Read 1 Corinthians 11:23-28.

What were Paul's instructions about the supper?

To prepare to take this sacred Lord's Supper, the Bible teaches, "Let a person examine himself" (1 Cor. 11:28) in his relationship with God and with others. If you are unsure of your salvation, may the Holy Spirit guide you as you read "Becoming a Christian" (p. 143). If you've been saved by faith in Jesus, ask yourself: "Am I trusting God by obeying His Word? Do I love God with all of my heart? Do I love others as myself?" Pray, thanking Jesus for reconciling you with God and close with the blessing from Hebrews 13:20-21.

Better than a keepsake tucked away, the bread and the cup are tangible reminders we share together to remember God's sovereign work throughout history, His unfailing love for us today, and His invitation to the final Lord's Supper.

For as often as you eat this bread and drink the cup, you proclaim the Lord's death until he comes.

1 CORINTHIANS 11:26

host a
Seder meal

by Larissa Arnault Roach

The *Seder* is the ritual meal those of the Jewish faith observe to commemorate Passover. Although the modern meal is not exactly like the meal Jesus and His disciples shared the night before His death, the rituals and meanings are similar. As followers of Christ, we can observe this meal as a way to better understand the Jewish heritage of our faith, plus we can make Christian application to many of the rituals. We can also use this time to point the way to true salvation in Jesus.

The traditional ceremony involves many complex elements, usually lasts three to four hours, and can feel overwhelming to a beginner. We're boiling the *Seder* down to the basics, so you can host an easy yet meaningful Passover meal.

1. **Plan the evening**. The *Haggadah*, a *Seder* guidebook, will explain the traditional songs, prayers, and schedule of events. But it's OK to include just some of the important elements of *Seder*. Simply choose a few readings and a few of your favorite worship songs. Check the library or find Jewish *Seder* traditions at www.chosenpeople.com/site/how-to-host-a-passover-seder/. There are also lots of resources out there that focus on Christ in the Passover or compare the Passover to the Lord's Supper.

2. **Arrange the room.** Cover a table with a white tablecloth. You will be situating all the *Seder* foods on the table as well as a traditional extra place setting for Elijah, the prophet who announced the Messiah's coming. Also, light two unscented white candlesticks on the table as a symbol of God's presence.

3. **Prepare the place settings.** For each participant, you'll need a dinner plate, a napkin, a glass filled with grape juice (in place of traditional wine), a fork, a spoon, a sprig of parsley, a small bowl of salt water, a hard-boiled egg, and a printout of any unfamiliar songs you plan to sing.

4. **Tell the Passover story.** Explain to your guests that *Seder* is part of the Passover holiday, one of the most important ancient Jewish festivals, ultimately pointing to the death and resurrection of Christ. Read the Passover story aloud from Exodus 12, then the last supper account from Luke 22:1-20.

5. **Serve the meal.** As the hostess, you'll prepare and then serve the symbolic foods at the heart of the *Seder* meal. Like other Jewish customs, *Seder* combines the physical and the spiritual in a multi-sensory experience. Together you'll taste foods that help you relive the Passover story. It's fun to have a Jewish cookbook on hand such as *Let My People Eat! Passover Seders Made Simple*, but you can easily find recipes for lamb and unleavened bread online. As you serve the different foods, explain each one's significance.

- PARSLEY symbolizes the hyssop dipped for sprinkling on the doorposts of Hebrew dwellings in preparation for the exodus. Instruct your guests to dip the parsley in the saltwater, taste it, and remember the tears shed in Egypt as well as the sorrow of Jesus dying on the cross. The green color also reminds us of the new life we have in Christ.

- HORSERADISH symbolizes the bitterness and harshness of Egyptian slavery. Invite guests to taste it, recalling how bitter their lives were when they were slaves to sin.

- HAROSET is a sweet mixture, made by grinding apples, nuts, and honey together that symbolizes the mud and straw the Israelites used in Egyptian construction. As everyone eats it, remember that Jesus is sweeter than honey.

- UNLEAVENED BREAD symbolizes the hurry in which the Israelites left Egypt—there wasn't enough time for the bread to rise. When mentioned in Scripture, yeast almost always represents sin. So as you eat the bread, meditate on Jesus as the Bread of life, our sinless sacrifice.

- GRAPE JUICE symbolizes Jesus' blood shed for us on the cross. Drink it in remembrance of Him.

- LAMB symbolizes the Passover lamb that was killed so its blood could be sprinkled on the doorposts of the Israelites' houses. This assured that the angel of death would pass over them. As you eat it, remember that Jesus is the Lamb of God who takes away the sins of the world.

- HARD-BOILED EGG symbolizes the cycle of life and endurance for the future.

6. **Close with sharing.** Invite your guests to share their perspectives on what Christ has done for them. Then wrap up singing worship songs together.

make room for
the King of kings

by Amanda Mejias

How often do you have to ask your teen to clean her room? Does it feel like you are daily asking your eighth grader to put his socks in the dirty clothes basket and not on the floor beside it? Or maybe you make all the other moms jealous because your teen loves organization and tidiness. Yeah, or maybe not.

Well, no matter where your teen's bedroom falls on the scale of clean living, you're going to want to put away the trash bags for now. You won't need them for the type of cleaning we're going to discuss in this activity.

The Passion Week should be all about making room in our hearts for Jesus. Therefore, if we want to clear out every obstacle and sin that hinders us from seeing Him clearly, we have some cleaning up to do.

As you prepare for Easter, plan an outing with your family to a favorite spot for coffee or dessert. Or order take-out and head to the park. Make sure to bring your family calendar and a journal with you. Use the time together to talk about your family priorities and discuss what may need to be readjusted. Ask questions like, "How can we spend more time together in God's Word as a family?" And "In what ways should we be serving our church and community better?"

Allow your teen to give input and make it a safe place for him to wrestle with how he can prioritize time with Jesus and serve Jesus over things like sleeping in, sports, and video games. But know, as the parent, you must lead the way and set the example for your teen. If your gym routine, Hulu® shows, or business meetings are coming before your relationship with Jesus, your teen will not only notice, he'll follow your lead.

So, let's clean our hearts of lesser things this week and help our families make room for the King of kings.

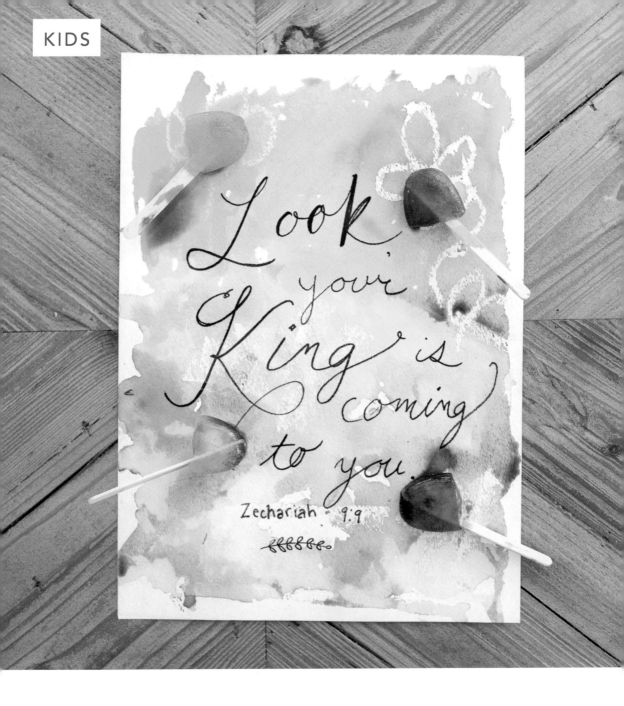

Look, your King is coming to you.

Zechariah 9:9

how to paint

Remembrance art

by Kayla Stevens

Long before Jesus was born, the prophet Zechariah prophesied that God would send the righteous and victorious King at the right time (Zech. 9:9). Jesus fulfilled this prophecy on Palm Sunday. Create remembrance art to help your family remember the events leading up to Jesus' death and resurrection.

GATHER

- ice tray
- food color (red, blue, yellow, and green)
- craft sticks
- heavy white paper and newspaper
- a permanent marker.

Note: Food color will stain fabric.

Place a few drops of food color into ice tray compartments. Fill the trays with water and gently stir the color to mix it well. As you do, discuss how the colors can remind your family of the important events of Jesus during this week.

Green represents the celebration of Palm Sunday as Jesus entered Jerusalem. Brown helps us to remember when Jesus turned over tables to stop people from misusing the temple. Blue reminds us that Jesus washed His disciples' feet to teach them about serving others and spiritual cleansing. Yellow reminds us of the bread Jesus broke at the last supper, and red represents the cup Jesus shared with His disciples at the last supper. During this meal, Jesus established the first Lord's Supper.

Place small craft sticks in each ice cube section and freeze the ice tray for six hours or overnight.

Write the hopeful words of Zechariah's prophecy on your art paper: "Look, your King is coming to you" (Zech. 9:9). Cover your workspace with newspaper. Then, remove the ice cubes and paint creative designs on your Scripture art paper. As the ice melts, the color transfers to your paper. Once your artwork is dry, place it in your home to remind you that Jesus is the promised King!

The Garden to the Tomb

WEEK 3

Behold Your King

By Sarah Doss

As you picked up this Bible study, did the subtitle *Behold Your King* sound familiar to you? We read these three words in John 19:14, spoken by Pilate to the Jews, just before they demanded that Jesus be killed.

The words *King of the Jews* were emblazoned on the sign that hung over Jesus on the cross as He drew fleeting breath and bore the agony of our sins. The King God's people had prayed for and begged God to send for years and years, had been betrayed in a single moment.

And yet, He remained their King.

And yet, He remains our King.

I'll level with you, this week's study isn't going to be easy. We are going to walk with Jesus through His time in the garden of Gethsemane and through the many "trials" where He was convicted of wrongdoing, though He remained sinless. We'll watch as Jesus is betrayed and abandoned by some of the people closest to Him. We'll read the account of Jesus on the cross, and imagine ourselves standing vigil as He suffered on our account. We'll journey with Nicodemus and Joseph of Arimathea as they bury Jesus' body and we'll sit in the sacred space of silent Saturday with the Marys who watched the great stone roll over the entrance of the tomb (Matt. 27:60-61), unsure of what was to become of their hope.

I know it's tempting to rush through these passages; it's natural to want to look away from the unimaginable hardship and pain that Jesus endured. But, this week, just this week, would you take the time to sit with these passages and let the gravity of the described events sink in for a moment?

As if you were sitting with a friend in grief, sit with Jesus in the silence. Pray that God would illuminate the Scripture to help you understand the events of this week and the sacrifice Jesus made in a deeper, more intimate, way.

Though we shy away from hardship and stories of deep pain, the reality is—as followers of Jesus who love Him and are loved by Him—these sufferings purchased our freedom. Read these words about Jesus, prophesied in Isaiah, years before Jesus came to earth:

> Yet he himself bore our sicknesses,
>
> and he carried our pains;
>
> but we in turn regarded him stricken,
>
> struck down by God, and afflicted.
>
> But he was pierced because of our rebellion,
>
> crushed because of our iniquities;
>
> punishment for our peace was on him,
>
> and we are healed by his wounds.
>
> ISAIAH 53:4-5

He bore our grief. He bore our pain. He had done no wrong. Yet, He sacrificed Himself so that we could know God, so that we could be with God and have life everlasting. He knew we could never make it on our own, so He did it for us. That's our King.

This week, I pray that the solemnity of these stories would fuel your grateful worship of God. As you consider the hardship that Jesus endured for you, may you behold your King with love and hope anew.

What was your favorite day of study this week? Why?

If you knew you only had one week left to live, what would you do during that week?

One of the things Jesus did in the last week of His life was teach on His second coming. When you think about Christ's return, does it frighten you or excite you? Explain. What preparation do you still need to make for His return?

One of the stories we looked at last week was Mary's expression of extravagant love for Jesus by anointing Him with perfume. Would you say you have extravagant love for Jesus? How do you express it? How can you?

Who do you know who has a servant's heart? Why did you choose this person? Would you consider yourself to have a servant's heart? Why or why not? Why is serving people such a reflection of Christ?

How often does your church take the Lord's Supper? Consider the last time you participated in this ordinance. Was it intensely meaningful, more of a ritual, or somewhere in between? Explain.

Close your time with prayer, asking God to show you the true condition of your heart. Ask Him to give you the heart of a servant—to give you eyes to see people as He sees them and be willing to sacrificially meet their needs.

THE PATH TO SUBMISSION: THE GARDEN OF GETHSEMANE

by Betsy Langmade

The last days of a believer's life are sacred. Especially when you know his or her final day is imminent. My mother had markers of leukemia in her blood for many years when suddenly her condition crossed over to acute leukemia. A few symptoms, a routine blood test, and there she was hearing the shocking diagnosis. When I arrived by her side, my siblings and I sat on the edge of her hospital bed and listened to the doctor deliver the news. "I'm sorry to tell you this but you have days, maybe weeks, to live." What? We stood to our feet in disbelief as tears rolled down our cheeks.

Twenty-three days later I watched my mother breathe her last breath. Those twenty-three days were spent in purposeful living. There were carefully planned moments to say and do the things that were most important. None of us wanted to leave anything undone, no words unsaid, no feelings unexpressed. It was incredibly sad. It was sacred.

Jesus' final days were marked with many memorable moments. His intent to prepare and pray for His disciples was evident, as seen in our previous day's study. His words and actions carried weight in the hearts and minds of His followers as they left the upper room.

Read Luke 22:39-53 and John 18:1-12.

Today we find ourselves experiencing, through our reading, the final days of Jesus' life on earth. Will you insert yourself in this narrative with me? Put on your sandals and let's walk with Jesus and His disciples from the upper room to the garden of Gethsemane. We'll be taking along our willful hearts, our nagging doubts, our confusion and fear—all of it goes to garden with us. Let's see what we will learn from Jesus as He prepares for His death.

We've walked a little over a mile with Jesus to get to the familiar place of prayer. Jesus and His disciples have been here many times. But this night there is a bit more mystery around what is taking place.

This time Jesus is asking more, feeling more, needing more. Three times He asks His friends to watch and pray for Him. Three times they fail. Jesus is overcome with sorrow, deeply distressed and burdened with the horror of what He is about to endure in the coming days.

So, He prayed "My Father" with depth of relationship no human will ever know. Remember that Jesus was fully God and fully man. As His knees buckled and He landed with a thud on the ground, His heart cried out in anguish, "if it is possible, let this cup pass from me. Yet not as I will, but as you will" (Matt. 26:39).

His words of submission confront us, slapping us in the face with a stinging wake-up call. We are awakened to a stunning display of utter selflessness and abandon.

Note how this moment is described in three Gospel accounts. As you read, write what is repeated in each one and what is unique to only one or two.

Matthew 26:36-46

Mark 14:32-42

Luke 22:39-42

What are your thoughts as we watch Jesus in these deeply intimate moments with the Father?

Familiarity. I find it so comforting that the first recorded word of Jesus' prayer in Luke is "Father." In Mark, it's recorded as "Abba, Father." Jesus is addressing His Father with the tenderness of a son. There is no hesitation, no qualifying, no pleading. Jesus just calls out His name with an assurance that the Father is there, watching and listening.

When is the last time you cried out to God as "Father"? Perhaps that's not easy for you. Ask Jesus to help you understand why. Ask Him to help you find the path to approach God as Father today. Talk to someone you trust about helping you navigate any obstacles you may have. Your Father is waiting for you with open arms.

> If you are comfortable with addressing God as Father in prayer, call out to Him now and share your deepest need with Him. Write your prayer below.

Jesus' honesty of heart in His prayer is an important example for us. The Gospels tell us that Jesus' heart was troubled, sorrowful, and in great anguish and distress (Matt. 26:37; Mark 14:33; Luke 22:44). He cried out to His Father with raw emotion. His full awareness of His circumstances drove Him to overflow with gut-wrenching, honest conversation with His Father.

In our most agonizing, emotional moments we, too, can come to God in full honesty. How silly of us to think that we can do anything else. Our Father sees the depth of our struggle.

> Describe a time when you were emotionally honest with God in prayer.

> What did you sense was God's response to you?

Paraphrasing Jesus' prayer might sound something like this: "Father, I understand fully what Your will is. I understand that it will not only mean my physical death, but also My carrying the weight of the sins of all humankind to the cross. I know that I must suffer physical pain, endure humiliation, set aside my power and do it willingly for Your glory."

In the Gospel accounts we see Jesus ask if there's another way, but then He submits to the Father's will with "not my will, but yours, be done" (Luke 22:42b).

Nothing in our human experience comes close to what Jesus wrestled with in the garden that night. But our response to His example should challenge us to confront our willfulness and plead for a heart of submission to His perfect will. Honest, intense prayer moves us to abandon our will and miraculously prefer and embrace His perfect will and purpose.

We live with stubborn hearts every day, tempted to follow our will, our way, to do what we want. Instead it should be His will, His way, to do what He wants. Here's the bottom line: we were not put on this earth to exercise our own will; we were put here to do the will of our Father.

> When have you recently struggled with your own willfulness? Did you cry out to God for the will to be submissive to Him? How did He meet you in that struggle? Write your thoughts below.

> If you are currently struggling to submit your will and have not yet cried out to God, do that now. Write out your conversation with Him below. Be honest about your struggle. Ask Him to fill you with the desire to do His will by the power of His Holy Spirit.

The garden where Jesus met with His Father is the same garden that holds a poignant event that propels Him to the cross.

Read the following passages and imagine yourself, once again, in the garden with Jesus. What you see will leave you astounded.

- Matthew 26:47-56

- Mark 14:43-50

- Luke 22:47-53

- John 18:1-12

At the last supper, Jesus predicted that Judas would betray Him (Matt. 26:20-25). After Jesus prayed His prayer of submission, suddenly a mob gathered around Him. Judas came and greeted Jesus with a kiss. Usually the kiss would have been a customary greeting of friends, or to show respect or allegiance. But this was a kiss of betrayal, a way to identify Jesus to the mob leaders.

But Jesus was already offering Himself up to the soldiers, chief priest, and officials, knowing that His arrest was God's will, leading to His imminent death on the cross. It's important for us to remember in this moment that Jesus was both fully God and fully man. While He possessed the power to save Himself, He chose the will of His Father in order to provide salvation for every human.

As Jesus gave Himself up, Peter lashed out at the priest's servant with his sword, cutting off the servant's ear (John 18:10). Immediately, Jesus reached out, touched the servant, and his ear was healed. I love this act of Jesus. In the midst of the chaos, accusation, and His arrest, Jesus was still seeing and meeting an individual's need. That moment should leave us awestruck. Jesus sees you today and longs to meet your deepest need.

I pray that the garden of Gethsemane will forever be a precious place to you. The place where our salvation was settled. It led Jesus to the cross where He took the swirling devastation and destruction of sin—all of it—on our behalf, so that we could receive God's saving grace and eternal hope.

JESUS' TRIALS AND PETER'S DENIAL

by Christina Zimmerman

During His Passion Week, Jesus spent His days teaching, but at night, He was secluded in prayer on the Mount of Olives (Luke 21:37). It was there that Jesus submitted to a mob of people who carried swords and clubs. Heavily influenced by the opinions of the religious leaders, Jesus was perceived by the mob to be guilty of acts that warranted a criminal's arrest and a criminal's trial. The three previous years Jesus spent in ministry—preaching and teaching, healing the sick, and setting the captives free—did not seem to matter.

Read Luke 22:47-53 to review the scene in the garden.

What do you believe was going through the minds of the different players in this scene—the mob, the religious leaders, the disciples, Jesus?

The atmosphere was hostile. The mob of people who arrested Jesus must have been vicious and angry. An audio of Jesus' arrest might reveal words that could not be read at a children's Bible story hour. Following His arrest, Jesus was led away to the house of Annas, the former high priest, who was the father-in-law of the current high priest, Caiaphas (John 18:12-13). At this point almost all of the disciples had scattered (Matt. 26:56). They assumed they would stand with their King, but human nature won out in the end. One disciple who remained was Peter. However, he followed at a distance, under the cloak of darkness. Circling around, he tracked down the arresting mob and remained silent. John 18:15 indicates that "another disciple" (probably John) also followed.

If you were confronted about your beliefs about Jesus, would your stance for Christ remain strong? Explain.

Read Luke 22:54-60.

The mob that waited outside of the house of Annas sat down in the courtyard around a newly lit fire. Peter sat there among them. But the light of the fire unveiled his face, and a servant recognized him. She said, "This man was with Him too." At this point, Peter had an opportunity to make things right with the Master, to reclaim his allegiance to the one he loved, but Peter's fear was too overwhelming. The lie rolled easily from his mouth, "Woman, I don't know Him."

A little later someone else pointed a finger at Peter, asserting he was one of the followers of Jesus. Peter again strongly denied it. But the accusations launched at Peter were not over. An hour later, another man, repeatedly addressed the crowd about Peter, saying, "This man was certainly with him, since he's also a Galilean." This was the strongest assertion of the night.

Peter was physically and emotionally exhausted and surrounded by unbelievers. With an empty spiritual well and nothing to draw from, Peter succumbed to his sinful flesh and again denied knowing Jesus.

Write down a time when you were so exhausted you followed your flesh rather than the Spirit of Christ.

Read Luke 22:61-65.

Just as Jesus predicted, Peter denied Him. When the rooster crowed, Jesus, who was nearby, turned and looked at Peter. At that point, Peter remembered what Jesus had told him as Jesus prepared His disciples for His farewell. John records in his Gospel that Peter eagerly told Jesus he would stay with Him, even if it cost him his life. But Jesus prophesied that Peter's good intentions would not hold when confronted with genuine danger (13:37-38). Filled with shame and guilt, Peter cried bitterly. Jesus knew exactly what Peter would do, but Jesus did not stop loving him. In the same way, when we do things that hurt Jesus, His love for us never changes. His love is unconditional, and He will forgive us when we ask (1 John 1:9).

Recall a time you denied Jesus. What were your emotions in that moment? How did you respond to the Spirit's conviction?

During the night of His arrest, Jesus was beaten and ridiculed. The guards mocked Jesus and played childish games with Him, trying to humiliate and anger Him. It was deep disrespect toward the One who held all power in His hands. The only charge they had against Jesus was blasphemy.

Read Luke 22:66–23:12.

The religious leaders brought Jesus to stand before the Sanhedrin at first light. When they questioned Jesus about being the Messiah or the Son of God, Jesus did not give them a direct answer. He recognized the trap they had set before Him and cleverly turned the questioning back on them. But He did unexpectedly point to Himself as the Son of Man, which placed Him next to God in heaven.[1]

This outraged the Sanhedrin. They claimed that Jesus made divine claims about Himself, and they pronounced Him guilty. No witnesses were called and no defense made on Jesus' behalf. (In both Matthew's and Mark's accounts, witnesses came forward but their testimonies didn't agree.) In the court's interpretation, Jesus had condemned Himself. Unknowingly, these humans convicted the One who would one day judge them. Also, unknowingly, they were on the way to glorifying Jesus on the cross.

Do you think God still accomplishes His will through people with evil intentions? If so, what does that say about the sovereignty of God?

Though the Sanhedrin condemned Jesus on religious grounds, they had no power to execute Him. Only the Roman ruler could do that. So the religious leaders took Jesus to Pilate, the Roman governor. Also, they knew the religious charge would not stand in Pilate's court, so they made up political charges: "He's a corrupt leader!" "He's a tax evader!" "He's leading a coup to make Himself King!" But Pilate found no grounds for charging Jesus. During the questioning, Pilate learned from the crowd that Jesus was a Galilean. He used this as a convenient way to excuse himself from the Sanhedrin's headhunt. He turned Jesus over to the jurisdiction of Herod Antipas, ruler over Galilee. Standing before Herod, Jesus refused to respond to Herod's questioning. He did not open His mouth. Herod simply ridiculed Him as a fake king and sent Him back to Pilate.

What emotion or response does the trial of Jesus evoke in you? How does Jesus' attitude during His trial settle your heart?

Read Luke 23:13-25.

Upon Jesus' return to his court, Pilate still found no reason to charge Him. Therefore, Pilate recommended that Jesus be whipped and released. Instead, the crowd insisted that Jesus die. Pilate thought he had an out. Every year at the Passover Festival, he had a practice of releasing one prisoner. He gave them the choice between Jesus, who was innocent of the charges, or Barabbas, a notorious criminal. The crowd chose Barabbas and cried out for Jesus to be crucified (Matt. 27:15-26). Despite all of Pilate's attempts to release Jesus, the angry crowd demanded Jesus' death. So Pilate, "wanting to satisfy the crowd" (Mark 15:15), did as the crowd demanded and handed Jesus over to be crucified.

Have you ever found yourself with a similar choice—satisfy the crowd or do the right thing? What choice did you make?

Jesus was savagely arrested, denied by His disciple, Peter, and unjustly tried by both Jewish and Roman authorities, but He was never convicted of a crime that deserved death. The legal system of today would still find no fault in Jesus. But just like the mob, the Sanhedrin, Pilate, and Herod, many people refuse to acknowledge Jesus as Messiah and Lord. How about you? Have you accepted Jesus as Lord of your life? Do your attitudes and actions give evidence of that decision? Consider today whether you stand with the crowd or apart from it.

THIS IS JESUS, THE KING OF THE JEWS

by Mary Wiley

Describe a time when you experienced a heavy consequence for sin.

The consequences of sin are weighty—so weighty that the just punishment for the breaking of God's instruction is death. In a season of celebrating Jesus' resurrection, I am often tempted to lessen the weight of the wrath of God and the penalty necessary to atone for sin. It's easy to skip the suffering of Good Friday and the deafening silence as our Savior lay in the grave.

In just three days following the suffering and cross, our Savior would be resurrected, demonstrating His defeat of sin and death. His sacrifice would prove the right atoning payment, securing the promise for all who trust Him to be raised as He was. The end is glorious, but the means to that end are bloody.

Today, we are going to take the time to mourn the death of our King who took on the wrath of God for our sin on the cross.

Read Matthew 27:27-56. What was the charge against Jesus?

What insults did the soldiers, those who passed by, the chief priests, the teachers of the law, the elders, and even those crucified beside Him use to mock Him?

Roman crucifixion was known as the most painful and humiliating method of execution, so gruesome it was not to be used on Roman citizens, no matter the crime. A person hung on a cross would not usually die due to wounds inflicted before the crucifixion, the carrying of the one hundred pound crossbeam along the longest route through the city (to discourage others from rebellion), or the nailing of the body to the cross. Instead, death ultimately came by asphyxiation as the muscle groups used to breathe became more and more weakened because of one's posture on the cross.[2]

Jesus, our Savior, was hung on a cross used for the most heinous criminals as a sinless man. The plaque above His head declared His crime, while also speaking the truth of His identity: He was the King of the Jews. He was mocked as if He could not save Himself, and yet, as God the Son, all-powerful over all creation, with legions of angels at His beck and call (Matt. 26:53), He continued in obedience to the Father, even to death on the cross.

> In Matthew 27:51-53, what occurred in the temple as Jesus breathed His last? In the land? In the holy city?

> Place yourself in the shoes of the onlookers that day: the ones who mocked or spit at Jesus, the soldiers who stood watch, or the dearly loved friends who stood at a distance. Describe how you might have reacted to these events.

When our Savior, the Light of the world, breathed His last, the curtain was torn, the earth shook, the rocks split, and graves were opened. People rose from the dead. While there are a lot of questions about what actually happened and when, we do have a picture of what Jesus accomplished: in His death and resurrection He is the firstfruits of what is to come, so our resurrection is secured (1 Cor. 15:20).

The temple had been the center of Jewish life since its advent, and the curtain between the holy place and the holy of holies, where God's presence specially dwelt, was torn from top to bottom.

This curtain separated the clean from the unclean, the holy from the profane. The holy of holies was the space that only the high priest could enter after much purification, and only once per year on the Day of Atonement (Lev. 16:11-28). Every element of this day was a reminder of God's holiness and humanity's need for pardon, and this is where we find an understanding of why Jesus had to die for sin.

According to Romans 3:23, what is the deserved consequence for sin?

God is holy, set apart, fully good, and without sin. God required holiness from His people as stated in the Law. To gain this holiness, the people's sin had to be atoned for through sacrifice. God's wrath for sin was palpable.

The sacrificial system the priests completed day in and day out in the temple, and especially on the Day of Atonement, made a way for God's wrath to be satisfied, but not once and for all. It was a constant reminder of death as the consequence of sin. The offering—often a spotless lamb or goat—would be burned on the altar, taking death on your behalf and atoning for your sin.

Read 2 Corinthians 5:21.

What does this passage say Jesus became for us?

On the cross, Christ became sin for us. He took on the wrath of the Father. Jesus was forsaken in our place so that we might not be forsaken by God because of our sin. Jesus swapped places with us, taking our deserved penalty and giving us His righteousness. He is our substitute. Righteousness could not be achieved by the Law, but only by the blood of the One righteous Lamb, Jesus (Gal. 2:21).

Read Romans 5:12-21.

Compare and contrast the sin brought by Adam and the grace brought through Jesus.

Flip back to Matthew 27. How did the centurion and those with him respond in verse 54?

Creation was proclaiming Jesus as Savior, and the first exclamation of truth after His death comes from a Gentile.[3] Jesus had not come to simply be the King of the Jews, but to be the way for all who would make Him King of their lives. He had come to live the righteous life Adam was incapable of living. He had come to secure the grace of God for all who would trust Him for salvation. He would destroy the temple (His body) and rebuild it in three days in His death and resurrection. He wouldn't save Himself from the suffering of the cross, but He would pay for sin so that all who trust Him would not suffer the eternal consequence of it. This is love, that He would be obedient to the point of the cross so that we might have life.

Write John 15:13 below and spend some time thanking God for what Christ has done for you.

Don't allow the weight of the wrath of God toward sin to be lost on you today. Spend some time confessing your sin and thanking God that He would send the One who alone can atone for our sin and apply His righteousness to our lives.

THE BURIAL OF JESUS

by Amanda Ozment

As we study the Easter passages year after year, we say the words "Jesus' death, burial, and resurrection" often. We spend a lot of time talking about the details leading up to and including His death. We talk about the stone being rolled away, the angels, the post-resurrection appearances, and so on. But what about the "in-between time?" What happened between the time Jesus was taken off the cross until He rose again? People had to step up in faith to make sure that Jesus' body was properly cared for. Ironically, some rather unlikely characters stepped up to the plate.

At around three o'clock in the afternoon on that Friday, the Savior of the world died. As modern believers, we are blessed not to have experienced that feeling of grief and sadness of seeing Him suffer on the cross. We know Him as our Savior who is very much alive. But, for approximately thirty-six hours, Jesus' spirit was thoroughly and properly gone from His earthly body. Blood was no longer flowing through His veins. The decomposition process had set in, just as it does in every person who dies. Plus, as the sun was about to go down, it was almost the Sabbath. Time was of the essence to take care of Jesus' body.

Read John 19:38.

Who took care of Jesus' dead body? Why is that surprising?

In the moments after Jesus' passing, we know there were several people looking on (Mark 15:40-41), but it was Joseph of Arimathea who jumped into action. Joseph was a prominent member of the Sanhedrin, the religious ruling class of the day. For someone of his class and stature to ask for the dead body of a criminal would have made him a social outcast. Even Jesus' inner circle of disciples were nowhere to be found at this point, afraid of the consequences they too might suffer. However, Joseph knew that his power combined with his faith was exactly what was needed at this moment.

Joseph's desire to step up to the plate actually fulfilled an Old Testament prophecy concerning what would happen to the Messiah's body at His death (See Isa. 53:9.)

 Though as a religious leader, Joseph would have no doubt been a scholar of the Scriptures, he was likely blissfully unaware of the role he was fulfilling. He was simply a believer who knew he had the power to do what was right in the moment and wasn't afraid to do it.

Read John 19:39-40.

Who was the other unlikely caretaker of Jesus' body? Where have we seen him before?

Nicodemus has now made his third appearance in the Gospel of John. In his first encounter with Jesus (John 3), he came with lots of questions. Nicodemus was a theologian—he knew the Scriptures; he knew the Jewish law, but he couldn't discount the signs in front of him. He had to talk to Jesus and figure out how this Rabbi fit into his own personal beliefs. The term "born again" comes from Nicodemus' encounter with Jesus, along with arguably the most recognized verse in all of the Bible—John 3:16.

Nicodemus made his second appearance in John 7. It seems some people saw Jesus' signs and wonders, listened to His teaching, and believed He was truly the Messiah. But there were doubters too, especially among the Pharisees. They wanted to arrest Him for His "false teaching," but Nicodemus stood up for Jesus saying, "Our law doesn't judge a man before it hears from him and knows what he's doing, does it?" (John 7:51) Whether Nicodemus was a follower of Christ at this time is unknown, but no doubt his previous encounter had him thinking. By the time we see Nicodemus joining Joseph in preparing Jesus' body, he was risking his reputation and status to help someone he believed in.

Read John 19:41-42 and Matthew 27:57-60.

What do these passages tell us about the tomb where Jesus was placed?

Joseph took Jesus' body to a new, unused tomb that he owned. These may seem like insignificant details, but these few sentences are critical to proving our faith to those who doubt the resurrection of Christ. There is proof that Christ was laid in the tomb dead, wrapped tightly in seventy-five pounds of spices, and laid to rest completely alone with a heavy stone rolled in front of the tomb's entrance. When the tomb was empty three days later, the only explanation was that Jesus had risen from the grave, just as He had said He would!

The burial of Jesus needed to be done properly. Joseph of Arimathea and Nicodemus took on this task despite their political, social, and even religious status within their community. Joseph's friends in the Sanhedrin likely knew what Joseph had done because it required going before Pilate to ask permission. Nicodemus gathered spices and aloes within the community to wrap Jesus' body. They weren't worshiping and helping Jesus in private. This was a public display of their faith in Christ.

Both of these men used their position to think through every detail, including asking permission for His body, making sure that His body was properly prepared, and ensuring He was buried with honor in a brand new tomb. Every step in this process was crucial, and they did it quickly and perfectly.

When was the last time you shared your faith in Jesus with someone outside of a church setting?

What hinders you from being more open about your faith?

Reflect today on what steps you can take to be more willing to share your faith and serve Christ openly. You may think what you can do for Jesus will be insignificant and not matter. But making Jesus known and serving the body of

Christ, His church, is vital, regardless of what role you fill.

A SILENT SATURDAY

by Amanda Mae Steele

When was the last time you or the environment around you was truly silent? I have found that it takes great intentionality for me to be silent. I instinctively reach for my phone, the remote, or a friend. And even if it appears that I'm working in silence, what isn't so obvious is the chatter of the voices in my mind.

But have you ever experienced a situation so big that it truly left you speechless? When the gravity of an event took your breath away, and the silence was so loud that you felt like you'd either explode or crumble?

Read Matthew 27:57-61.

Who watched Jesus be buried?

The two Marys sat near His lifeless body, despondent yet devoted, their hopes and dreams crushed. Which do you think was worse, to have to watch it all play out for hours, or to witness the finality of Jesus' death as the stone was rolled to seal His tomb?

And the timing of it all. Would the beginning of the Sabbath be a relief? After all, God designed the Sabbath to be a day of rest and a reminder of God's provision. If they were to honor their Master and be good Jews, the Marys would have wanted to observe the Sabbath, which also meant they couldn't give action to their grief during it. There would be no tending to His body, no to-do list to tend to at home to distract themselves, and no denying Jesus was dead.

We know the rest of the story. We know what they would find early on that Sunday morning. But they didn't. For all they knew, the One they'd put their hope in was gone. Forever.

We have God's Word which is holy, infallible, and complete. Our lives and our stories, however, are still being written before our eyes. Though we have our hope in Christ for eternity, and our abundant lives in Him today, there are still moments in our stories that are difficult, painful, and sorrowful. Times when it feels like God is silent.

> When have you walked through a time where God seemed silent? Perhaps it was a time of grief, confusion, or great disappointment. How did you handle that time? What did you learn? Take a moment to journal your thoughts about that season.

> Perhaps you're currently in a season of waiting, a time where God's will and voice are unclear. What has this season been like for you?

> Why do you think God allows or takes us through these times?

So often waiting is used for preparation and to gain new perspective. Perhaps your Saturdays of waiting were followed by a Sunday of celebration, just like the Marys experienced. Whatever the case, nothing is wasted with God. The silence has a purpose.

In our loud and noisy world, we need to sit in the silence at times. We purposefully made this day shorter to allow you to spend some time in silence before God.

If you're currently in a quiet season, invite the Holy Spirit to sit in silence with you (set a timer if that would be helpful) and allow yourself to rest in His arms just as you are. Ask the Holy Spirit to help you see the gifts the silence offers and to graciously receive them. And remember, sister: weeping may endure for the night, but joy comes in the morning (Ps. 30:5).

However, if life is good for you at the moment, still take some time to rest in silence today. Meditate on where we are in the passion story. Reflect on Christ's sacrifice and feel the weight of His work for you in the past and His work in you now.

After your time of silence, jot down a few thoughts, or a prayer, in the space below.

reflective hike

ideas

by Larissa Arnault Roach

This was a serious and somber week of study as we walked with Jesus to the cross. Consider finding an uncrowded place to take a reflective hike to think on what Christ has done for us.

Begin your hike with a still spirit, positioning yourself to hear from God. Select a verse or passage that stood out to you from this week of study to meditate on while walking. Or find some of the following items in nature to remind you of the week's events and help you process Jesus' sacrifice:

- Consider the time of day you're walking. If it's morning, meditate on Mark 15:1—*As soon as it was morning, having held a meeting with the elders, scribes, and the whole Sanhedrin, the chief priests tied Jesus up, led him away,* and handed him over to Pilate. If you walk in the afternoon, reflect on Mark 15:33-34—When it was noon, darkness came over the whole land until three in the afternoon. And at three Jesus cried out with a loud voice, "Eloi, Eloi, lemá sabachtháni?" which is translated, "My God, my God, why have you abandoned me? If it's an evening walk, consider Matthew 27:57-58 (ESV)—When it was evening, there came a rich man from Arimathea, named Joseph, who also was a disciple of Jesus. He went to Pilate and asked for the body of Jesus. Then Pilate ordered it to be given to him.

- Find a tree or bush with thorns or sharp pointy leaves, carefully touch the barbed portion and think on John 19:2-3—The soldiers also twisted together a crown of thorns, put it on his head, and clothed him in a purple robe. And they kept coming up to him and saying, "Hail, king of the Jews!" and were slapping his face.

- Pick up a heavy stick and carry it for several steps. Reflect on Isaiah 53:4a—Yet he himself bore our sicknesses, and he carried our pains. Or John 19:17-18—Carrying the cross by himself, he went out to what is called Place of the Skull, which in Aramaic is called Golgotha.

There they crucified him and two others with him, one on either side, with Jesus in the middle.

- Find a rock, boulder, or stone wall and meditate on Mark 15:46— After he bought some linen cloth, Joseph took him down and wrapped him in the linen. Then he laid him in a tomb cut out of the rock and rolled a stone against the entrance to the tomb.

- Somewhere toward the end of your hike, find a flower to remind you of what followed after the darkness of the cross. Meditate and celebrate the words of the angels "Why are you looking for the living among the dead?" ... "He is not here, but he has risen!" (Luke 24:5-6)

More Hike Ideas

- Hold on to this reflective time by taking photos, journaling, drawing your experience, or collecting small items of nature along the way.

- Use a voice notes app on your phone to speak what you are learning from God.

- Select the verses in a Bible app and play them audibly while you hike.

surrendering

your will

by Amanda Mejias

"Not my will, but yours." Have you ever found yourself in a desperate situation praying similar words to the ones Jesus prayed in Luke 22:42?

It's so easy to hold things like our family, our health, our future, and our comfort with closed fists. Our finite minds convince us that if we surrender our desires to God, we will compromise our security and our joy. But Scripture reveals the opposite is true, and Jesus Himself displays the rewarding treasure to be found in humbly submitting to the Father.

At any point on the way to the cross, Jesus could have halted the process. He could have changed His mind. He could have shunned the sacrifice. Jesus could have forsaken us. But, He embraced the cross and His death with full humility because He trusted the heart of the Father.

Open your Bible and read Philippians 2:5-11. Invite your teen to join you in reading that passage, and then discuss what the humility of Christ that led Him to the cross has to do with surrendering our wills to God.

Ask your teen to share what this kind of surrender might look like in her life—facing things such as college decisions, upcoming tryouts, a relationship, and so on.

List the situations and decisions your teen expresses. Create your own list of circumstances you're dealing with, then together, pray over both lists, humbly asking the Lord for His will to be done.

If we can trust God to be faithful at the cross, we can trust Him to be faithful in every other aspect of our lives.

make a
Cross of Beauty

by Kayla Stevens

Jesus understood the suffering He would endure for humanity. His obedience to God and His love for us led Him to suffer and die to save us from our sin and restore our relationship with God.

Work with your family to cover a cross. As you do, talk about why Jesus had to suffer and die.

GATHER

- a small piece of cardboard
- a craft knife or scissors
- a dark-colored marker
- different patterns of decorative tape

Cut a cross shape out of cardboard, and invite your family to think about how they've disobeyed God through their thoughts, words, or actions. Explain that anything we think, say, or do that goes against what God says is sin. With younger children, allow them to color the cross completely with a dark-colored marker to represent the sin we all commit. With older children, consider asking them to write different sins they have committed on their cross shape.

Remind your kids that everyone sins. (See Rom. 3:23.) We have sinful hearts that want to choose sin instead of obeying God. The punishment we all deserve because of our sin is death, but Jesus died to take that punishment for us. His death covered all of our sins and made a way for us to be forgiven and saved. Through Him we have the gift of eternal life (Rom. 6:23).

Invite children to use decorative tape to cover the cross completely. Talk with your family about how Jesus covered our sin when He died on the cross. When we look at the cross, we can remember that our sins have been covered by the beauty of Jesus' sacrifice and love. When we trust in Jesus, our sins are forgiven!

He is Risen!

Bright Hope for Tomorrow

by Sarah Doss

When we last met, we left two Marys at Jesus' tomb, sorrowful and silent, waiting. It strikes me that many of the seasons of our lives are marked by waiting, by feelings of solitude. We often feel left alone with our longings, unmet hopes or desires.

The good news of the gospel, and the good news of our study this week is that God never leaves His children alone. He promises to never leave us or forsake us, even in the most difficult times.

As you may know, the solemnity of Silent Saturday was met with the best news the world has ever heard. Jesus rose from the dead on Sunday, defeating death and the grave forever. He's alive today, sitting at the right hand of God the Father making intercession for us. He's Lord over our lives and He's Lord over sin and death. He has the final say on all things—so He has the final say on our eternal security—life with Him forever. But, I'm getting carried away.

This week, we're going to discuss Jesus' appearing to many of His followers after His resurrection. (Wouldn't you have loved to have been a fly on the wall when Jesus made His first appearance? Can you imagine the expressions on His followers' faces? I imagine it to be pure joy and confusion all at once.) We'll watch as Jesus forgives Peter for denying Him and restores the sometimes bumbling disciple (Don't we all identify with Him sometimes?) to the work of kingdom ministry.

We're going to take some time to really unpack how and why the resurrection matters for those of us who follow Jesus thousands of years after His resurrection. And we're going to finish out our study this week by focusing on Jesus' last commands to His followers before He ascended to heaven.

Yes, we've got a lot of ground to cover, but I'm glad to say, after the grief we walked through last week, this journey is bursting with light and hope to spare.

As we launch into this week of study, take time to consider what these moments would have been like for Jesus' followers. After following the man they believed to be the Messiah for years, He was suddenly gone. They must have wondered what was to become of them or the truth that Jesus had taught them. Where should they go from here? Should they just walk back to their fishing nets and families and homes and forget the whole thing?

Confusion, hopelessness, and despair—had it all been for naught?

And then, on the first day of the week, a weeping Mary was met by a man who called her by name, whom she immediately recognized as Jesus.

Several of the disciples went fishing and were hailed by a strange figure on the shoreline. This man gave them some fishing tips and after a night full of striking out, they hauled in more fish than they could pull out of the water.

Some disciples were locked away, fearing the Jews would harm them just as they had harmed Jesus. But then Jesus appeared to them saying, "Peace be with you. As the Father has sent me, I also send you" (John 20:21b).

Their fear and despair turned into joy and purpose. Their lives would never be the same again.

And Jesus does the same for us. He comes to us in our fear and uncertainty and brings peace. He comes to us in our restlessness and brings purpose.

Jesus is alive and that changes everything about our tomorrows.

What day of study was your favorite this week? Why?

Do you have a special place you go to pray? Where is it and why is it special?

Jesus submitted His will to the Father's purpose—"Not my will but yours, be done" (Luke 22:42). When was a time you struggled to submit your will to the Father's plan? What held you back? What was the outcome of your struggle?

What caused Peter to deny he knew Jesus? How does fear affect your walk with Christ and your witness for Him? How do you overcome that fear?

When you think about Jesus' suffering before and during the crucifixion, what is the most difficult part of this story for you? Why? If an unbeliever were to ask you why Jesus had to die, and in such a cruel way, what would you say?

Consider those you know who don't know Christ or understand His sacrifice for them. Take time to pray for them, that their hearts would be tender to the gospel. Tell God your willingness to share His story with those you've mentioned.

DAY 1

LOSING JESUS, FINDING JESUS

by Paige Clayton

If you could have one person back in your life whom you dearly loved and lost, who would it be?

Try to imagine if someone you loved more than anyone else died and was buried and then they appeared to you three days later, *alive!* How utterly amazing would that be?

Mary Magdalene's encounter with Jesus on the morning He rose from the grave was nothing short of astonishing. Even if you think you know this story well, let's try to experience it with a new perspective because this is not just a story. It really happened.

Read John 20:1-18. Then read it again aloud.

In your mind's eye, let the scene play out as if it were in a movie.

What, if any, lines, images, or phrases stand out to you?

This incredible encounter of Jesus and Mary Magdalene is one of my favorite interactions Jesus had with His followers on earth. It is powerful and tender and reveals the kindness of Jesus.

What does this encounter communicate to you about the heart of Jesus?

I wonder if Jesus let Mary be the first to see Him after He arose because He knew she needed it most.

If you have lost a loved one, you know the terrible pain and despair you experience just after that person dies. You're in shock and your memories can be blurry. But then what if suddenly, a few days later, you saw them and held them again? Can you imagine that? What would you do?

If I would have seen my father alive a few days after his death and heard him say my name, I think I might have fainted. I dreamed of that moment so many times.

Based on what you have read in the passage, what emotions was Mary likely feeling?

Grief displays powerful emotions and is a process. When Mary came to the tomb to anoint Jesus' body with spices, she was mourning Him intensely and doing what she could to still serve Him. She lost Him but she also lost what "might have been" with Him as the Messiah and King. Mary also experienced the trauma of watching Him die in agony.

Read Matthew 27:55-61.

Mary Magdalene was among the women who followed Jesus during His days of ministry on the earth. And she was there when He died. Then she, along with another Mary, watched Joseph of Arimathea put Him in the tomb.

In reading this, you might wonder why she was so devoted to Him. Read Luke 8:2-3 and describe how Jesus helped Mary Magdalene.

What else does this passage describe about Mary Magdalene?

Jesus had freed her from the torment of seven demons. The Bible does not tell us when or how that happened but He had literally rescued her. In turn, she followed Him in her life and even in His death. And that morning at the tomb, in the middle of her despair, the voice she knew well and loved, the voice she had heard teaching her so many times, the Savior who had freed her from torment *spoke her name!* *"Mary."* And everything changed.

What was Mary's response to Jesus speaking her name? (See John 20:17 for the implied action.)

She clung to Him! (Matthew's account tells us that she was holding on to His feet and worshiping Him [Matt. 28:9].) His gentle instruction for her to let go of Him, meant she must have been hanging on for dear life. She could not keep Him there because He had another purpose, and she could not relate to Him as she had. However, there's a beautiful juxtaposition in that moment—Jesus was taking care of her overwhelming individual need, yet at the same time moving toward taking His place at the right hand of the Father, thus finishing the mission of rescuing her and all of humankind from sin and death. What a beautiful Savior! Jesus is always both our saving King and Good Shepherd. We can cling to Him in our sorrow, in our joy, in our soul-piercing grief—and He will be with us. Even if we let go, He will not.

Describe a time in your life when you clung to Jesus and felt His comforting presence.

Because of Jesus, Mary's torment ended, and her grief turned to joy. Because of Jesus, I made it through the loss of my earthly father. Because of Jesus, my father and I both have salvation and will see each other again.

Because of Jesus' finished work on the cross and His resurrection, all who trust in Him will be saved. Though His work has sweeping ramifications for all people for all of eternity, this tender moment in the garden with Mary shows the heart of Jesus to love the one. To meet the need of the broken. To give hope to the despairing. He met Mary where she was. He stands ready and able to meet your every need also.

JESUS APPEARS TO THE DISCIPLES

by Bekah Stoneking

One of my favorite things about making brownies happens during the in-between—that time after I've poured the batter into the pan, but before the brownies are finished baking. During the in-between is when I get to lick the spoon (and during the in-between, raw eggs can't hurt me).

Read Luke 24:13-35.

Brownie batter smells delicious. Brownie batter tastes delicious. And a brownie-batter-covered-spoon is evidence of something fantastic: *brownies are coming!* As much as I love that in-between taste, it's ultimately just a foretaste of a better something that's on its way.

But that pesky "on its way" part frustrates me. I've had a taste. I know it's good. I know how I expect things to turn out in the end. But the spoon is licked clean and the dishes are washed up, and I have nothing but a watering mouth and unmet expectations because the brownies are still baking.

Does licking the spoon whet your appetite for the dessert that is to come? Or does it let you down because you had a taste of something wonderful, but now it's gone? Does it make you run back to the oven to curiously take a peek at the progress?

On that first Easter morning, Peter was one who ran back to get a look at what was happening. He, along with the other disciples, had heard the women's unbelievable testimony of the empty tomb and he just had to get a taste for himself (Luke 24:12). But some of Jesus' other followers needed more convincing.

In Luke 24:13-24, we find two despairing disciples commiserating over Jesus' crucifixion and the time that had passed since His death. Their anguish continued even after Jesus came near and began journeying with them. The text doesn't say whether the men were too upset to realize who they were talking to, or if God supernaturally concealed Jesus' identity, or if Jesus' resurrected body was just that unrecognizable. But whatever the case, their eyes were prevented from seeing Him clearly and they had no peace.

Despite all the evidence they had—solid knowledge of the Scriptures, the Law, and the Prophets, time spent physically with Jesus during His ministry, all the warnings and explanations He gave them, and the foreknowledge of the empty tomb—they were still foolishly slow to believe (v. 25).

You may find yourself wanting to shake these foolish followers by their shoulders for their unbelief. But if we're being fair and honest with ourselves, haven't we each been here before? Surrounded by different types of evidence of God's presence and work, but still riddled with fear, questions, and seemingly unmet expectations?

> What are some things that—despite evidence to the contrary—you still struggle to trust about God's character, His promises, or His good purposes for your life?

Jesus didn't shake the disciples. In the midst of their sadness, unmet expectations, doubt, and cloudy vision, Jesus dealt with them patiently.

In Luke 24:30, it says that when Jesus broke the bread and gave it to them, instantly the disciples eyes were opened. Finally, they recognized Him!

Why did it take so long? We know Jesus' character is not malicious, so we know He wasn't teasing the disciples. And we can assume His delay wasn't simply for the sake of giving us a good story to read. No, there is something more meaningful in the suppertime revelation. Perhaps God used this moment to open their eyes to see that the Bread of life that had been broken for them was now alive.

When we come to the table for the Lord's Supper, this is our way of remembering Christ and declaring His death and resurrection until He returns. But this practice is also for us. The habit of tasting and remembering brings us back to the main thing. It reveals the reality of the crucified and resurrected and one-day-returning Jesus over, and over, and over again. It reminds our finite brains of the promise of what's to come. It's even better than licking the spoon and smelling the baking brownies!

What are some ways you can combat doubt and fight to see the Lord more clearly? What rhythms in church life, fellowship with other believers, or personal devotion help you know God and trust Him?

Psalm 22:3 says that God inhabits or is enthroned on the praises of His people. Even if your heart is unsure and your voice is shaky, offer a word of praise to the Lord and trust that He is there in that moment.

After Jesus dealt patiently and lovingly with His disciples—even inviting Thomas to examine His wounds and touch Him (John 20:24-28)—Jesus spoke peace over them. He didn't condemn their questions or fears, challenge them, or mock their needs. Rather, Jesus took it upon Himself to make Himself known and then He lavished peace upon His followers. The disciples beheld Jesus and rejoiced in Him. This is *shalom*—life that is rightly ordered and reconciled to God, flourishing and abounding in peace. This is life as it should be.

Look at Luke 24:36-40 and John 20:19-29. Make note of each of Jesus' actions. What does His response to His disciples reveal about His character? What might this mean for His heart toward you?

Does this change your understanding of doubts, questions, struggles, or unmet expectations? If so, how?

What implications do Jesus' interactions with His disciples have for you and the way you interact with people who struggle to trust Jesus?

Being in Jesus' presence transformed the disciples. Christ transformed their questions, stress, confusion, and sorrow into *shalom*. Just as Jesus calmed the stormy sea (Matt. 8:23-37), He can calm our stormy souls. He is inviting you to be still in His presence, to obtain life, and to enter into everlasting acceptance with the Father. Behold: This is peace. This is your King. Taste and see.

During the time in between His resurrection and ascension, Jesus prompted His followers to question, think, examine, and believe. Or in more simple words—to taste and see. And today, during this time in between His ascension and His anticipated return to earth, He's inviting us to do the same.

This week, pull out your bowl and preheat your oven. After you mix up a batch of brownies and find yourself in the in-between, lick the spoon and meditate on these Scriptures you've studied today. Thank Jesus for the ways He patiently, lovingly, and exceedingly made Himself known to His followers. Journal about the ways He has made Himself known to you. Praise God for these things and allow your affections to be stirred at these foretastes of what is to come in heaven.

Smell the brownies as they bake. As your mouth waters and you anticipate the timer going off, allow this to turn your thoughts to the day when your faith will be made sight. As best as you can today, behold your King and worship Him for who He is and for the promises He made that you can confidently know will come true.

And when the brownies are finished baking, do what the disciples did. Invite someone else to taste and see. Over dessert with a friend, talk about how your heart burned within you as you studied God's Word. Tell her about what you discovered as you reached out and experienced Jesus. Follow Jesus' example and give your friend the loving freedom to examine and ask questions. Pray for God's Holy Spirit to open your minds to understanding the Lord all the more. Together, experience the warm goodness of living in Christ and following Him, because this is life. This is *shalom*.

JESUS RESTORES PETER

by Tessa Morrell

Everyone loves a good restoration story. Whether it's an old piece of furniture sanded and painted to look brand new, or a historic home brought back to its original glory through sweat and tears, we love to see broken things restored. I think it's because in our broken and hurting world, we long to see things made right. At peace. Whole again.

Take a minute and turn back to Week 3, Day 2 and review what you learned last week as you studied about Peter's denial of Jesus in Luke 22:54-62.

Remember that Peter "wept bitterly" at the realization that he had denied his Lord three times.

In the hours that followed his denial, as Jesus hung on the cross and died, do you think Peter believed his relationship with Jesus could be restored? Why or why not?

How did the reality of the resurrection of Jesus give Peter hope for restoration?

Read John 21:1-3.

Answer the following questions to take note of the setting and characters in this particular story in chapter 21.

Who was present, where were they, and what were they doing?

In John's Gospel, Jesus made three post-resurrection appearances to His disciples. John 21 records the final one. At this point, some of the disciples had left Jerusalem and returned to the Sea of Tiberias, which was another name for the Sea of Galilee. In nearly every conceivable way, their lives had been flipped upside down as they witnessed the arrest, death, burial, and resurrection of their dear friend and Rabbi, Jesus. Perhaps what felt most right and comforting at this time was simply returning to their roots in the area they grew up and doing the work they had always known—fishing on the Sea of Galilee.

Continue reading John 21:4-14.

The disciples fished all night long, but they didn't catch anything. By the time the sun began to rise over the sea, they were likely feeling tired and discouraged. That's when they heard someone call out to them from the shore. "Friends, you don't have any fish, do you?"

At this point, the men didn't know who had called out to them, but they simply replied no to this stranger who had stated the obvious.

"Cast the net on the right side of the boat, and you'll find some." When they did, they caught so many fish in their net that they couldn't haul it in.

That's when it started to click. John was the first to recognize Jesus. Then, splash! Peter plunged into the water and headed for the shore while the other disciples made their way in the boat.

What do you think made Peter jump into the water and head straight for the shore where Jesus stood?

Jesus invited the disciples to bring some of the fish they had caught and join Him for breakfast around a charcoal fire He had built on the beach.

As they ate, I wonder if the disciples felt a sense of normalcy return. After all, they had eaten countless meals together over the years they had lived and ministered alongside Jesus. Even with all they had gone through, it likely brought some peace to their hearts to simply share a meal with their Lord.

What is it about sharing a meal that brings people together?

Read John 21:15-25.

After breakfast, Jesus turned His attention to Peter. It seems that Jesus had already appeared to Peter three times before this encounter, twice when He was with the other disciples (John 20:19-29) and perhaps once just to Peter (1 Cor. 15:5).

What was the significance of Jesus asking Peter "Do you love me?" three times?

Verse 17 tells us that Peter was "grieved" that Jesus asked him a third time if he loved Him. At first, it may have felt like Jesus didn't believe him when he answered yes the first two times. However, it seems that Jesus was intentional about why He asked Peter to affirm his love and commitment to Him three times. Perhaps He was giving Peter the opportunity to affirm his love for each instance of denial that had taken place during Jesus' trial.

Notice that Jesus not only asked Peter to affirm his love. He also gave Peter an assignment.

What did Jesus ask Peter to do and what did the calling mean?

In John 10:11, Jesus said, "I am the good shepherd. The good shepherd lays down his life for the sheep." Jesus had demonstrated His love for His sheep—for humanity—by dying on the cross and rising from the grave. Now He was entrusting Peter with the role of caring for the flock.

In John 21:18-19, Jesus turned the conversation to describe the kind of death Peter would endure. According to tradition, Peter was sentenced to be crucified, but he insisted he be crucified upside down so that he wouldn't be put to death exactly like his Lord.

At the end of their conversation, Jesus gave Peter one last command in both verses 19 and 22, "Follow me." I wonder if those words in that setting flashed a vivid memory for Peter. Approximately three years before this encounter, Jesus had used the same words on this seashore to invite Peter to be His disciple (Mark 1:16-18). Their relationship had come full circle and was now restored in every way. It didn't mean the denial never happened, but it meant that Peter was forgiven, loved, and commissioned by Jesus in spite all that he had done. Nothing Peter did could take away Jesus' faithful friendship.

Through Jesus' finished work on the cross He initiated and provided a way of restoration to each of us. He invites us into His family through the gift of salvation (John 1:12-13).

> Have you professed your faith in Jesus and received Him as Savior and Lord? If so, write a couple of sentences here that summarize your experience. But If you've never put your faith in Jesus, you can do so right now. Please see page 143 for more information on how to become a Christian. Feel free to write your prayer of faith in the space below. Then tell a Christian friend about your decision.

Our relationship with Christ can never be broken. But in this life on earth we will still struggle with sin and disobey God at times, which breaks our fellowship with Him. It's important to be mindful of our sin and confess it to the Lord. He is always faithful to forgive, just like He forgave Peter (1 John 1:9).

> Are there currently areas of sin that you need to confess to the Lord? Write out a prayer of confession to Him.

While you're still breathing, it's not too late to experience restoration with Jesus. He will forgive and restore you as you call out to Him.

WHY JESUS' RESURRECTION MATTERS

by Kelly D. King

On the morning of December 7, 1941, Pearl Harbor, home to a United States naval base, was attacked without warning, killing more than 2,400 men and women. The attack propelled the United States into World War II. The following day, President Franklin D. Roosevelt, stood before Congress and declared December 7, "a date which will live in infamy."[1] It would also be the day my grandfather enlisted in the Navy and would serve in the South Pacific for the remainder of the war. For him, that date was personal and unforgettable.

Infamy is roughly translated "fame gone bad." In that now unforgettable speech, it might be hard to believe Roosevelt's first draft of the speech read, "a day which will live in world history."[2] One word mattered.

For Christians, there is a more important day in world history—the day Christ conquered death and was resurrected. Unlike a day of infamy, it is the most famous day in history, carrying the most important message of victory to all humankind, a hope of our own resurrection and power over death. The one word that mattered more, then and now, is *resurrection*. For believers, the resurrection of Christ is personal and unforgettable.

> If you had to pick a day in your lifetime that is often remembered, what would it be? How did that moment personally affect you?

In the past couple of days, you've examined some of the first appearances of the resurrected Christ. You've seen the tender appearance of Jesus with Mary at the tomb, how He appeared to the disciples, and how He restored Peter over a campfire on the shore of the Sea of Galilee. Yet, there is no other passage of

Scripture that gives more evidence of the importance of the resurrection than 1 Corinthians 15. Paul's treatment of the doctrine of the resurrection explains why it is the most pivotal point in history.

Some first-generation Christians not only believed the resurrection was crucial for history and for the gospel, but they experienced the resurrection as eyewitnesses.

Read 1 Corinthians 15:1-11.

What did Paul say was most important in verses 1-4, and why were these words most important?

Paul wanted the Corinthians (and us) to understand clearly the heart of the gospel—Christ's death, burial, and resurrection. Then Paul reinforced the truth of the last of these important events.

The testimony of reliable eyewitnesses as evidence in a court of law is vitally important today. It was even more important in the early church as evidence of the bodily resurrection of Christ. Paul provided a list of eyewitnesses to this miraculous event.

List the eyewitnesses from verses 5-8.

All of these people saw the risen Christ. From Peter, who would preach the resurrection in his first sermon at Pentecost (Acts 2) to Paul's own encounter on the road to Damascus (Acts 9), there were numerous occasions when people encountered the resurrected Jesus. And to bolster the credibility of the event, Paul included the only mention of Jesus appearing to five-hundred brothers and sisters at one time, many who were still alive when the letter was written.

Why were these eyewitness accounts vital to the spread of the gospel?

Why is Paul's account of eyewitnesses still important today?

First-generation Christians not only believed the resurrection was crucial for history, but they died because of it. They knew that the resurrection defeated death once and for all and that they, too, would experience resurrection. So they were unafraid to share the gospel despite the cost.

Despite the many witnesses to Christ's resurrection, evidently there were those in Corinth who disputed the resurrection of the dead. In response, Paul outlined several things that could be argued if the resurrection were not truth.

Read 1 Corinthians 15:12-19.

If there's no resurrection from the dead, and if Christ has not been raised from the dead then what would be the result?

• Verse 13:

• Verse 14:

• Verse 15:

• Verse 17:

• Verse 18:

• Verse 19:

Sounds pretty discouraging, doesn't it? Basically, if the resurrection is not true, we've wasted our lives and we're hopeless. However, Paul started 1 Corinthians 15:20 with a small, yet important word—*but*!

Read verses 20-22.

What was Paul's statement of truth and what are the promises that follow?

What does it mean that Christ is the firstfruits?

The firstfruits was the first part of the harvest to be brought in. It provided the certain hope that more was to come. Christ's bodily resurrection is the guarantee each of us has for our own resurrection. Paul's defense wasn't just about Christ's bodily resurrection, but it was the promise for every believer that we all will be raised with Him to eternal life.

Have you experienced resurrection power by putting your trust in Jesus Christ for your eternity? As was stated in yesterday's study, if you've never taken this step of faith, you can pray right now and ask the Lord to forgive you of your sins, place your trust in Him, and follow Him. If you have questions or would like more information, call a friend who is a believer or find a Bible-believing church in your area that can help you take the next step.

Finish today's study by reading 1 Corinthians 15:50-58.

Fill in the blanks of this glorious truth from verses 54-57.

Death has been swallowed up in _____. Where, death, is your _____? Where, death, is your _____? The sting of death is _____, and the power of sin is the _____. But thanks be to God, who gives us the victory through our Lord Jesus Christ!

My grandfather lived through World War II and experienced the thrill of victory. At the time, he was not a Christ follower. He would come to faith in Christ a few years later after being confronted with the death of a young man killed in a farming accident. As he faced his own mortality, my grandfather found true victory in a relationship with Christ. He lived the rest of his life in anticipation of Christ's return and so should we.

These promises written to first-century believers continue to encourage every believer to be steadfast, immovable, always excelling in the Lord's work. Though our current bodies will someday perish, as believers we will one day receive an imperishable body and live with Christ forever.

JESUS' PARTING WORDS AS HE ASCENDED INTO HEAVEN

by Rachel Forrest

Saying goodbye to a loved one is hard. Depending on the circumstances, there may be feelings of joy mixed with the sadness of loss. In the last year, I've learned just how difficult saying goodbye can be. My dad passed away in early 2019, and the journey of grief has been one of the most arduous roads I've ever walked.

While I thought my grief for my dad was unparalleled, watching my five-year-old son say goodbye has been even harder. Just this week, he crept into our bedroom well after bedtime, tears in his eyes, and he lamented how much he misses his papa. In between sobs and sniffs, he said, "I just want him to come down from heaven and see me right now." He was papa's "little buddy," and while he is filled with the hope that he'll see his papa again one day, he aches for that sweet reunion and doesn't understand why he can't have that now.

I imagine that Jesus' dear friends experienced similar emotions on the day of His ascension.

Read Luke 24:36-49 and Acts 1:1-4.

Jesus made several appearances to His followers in the forty days after His resurrection. During that time, the Gospel writer Luke tells us that Jesus "opened their minds to understand the Scriptures" (Luke 24:45), helping them to see how He was the fulfillment of all the Old Testament promises for their coming Messiah and spoke to them "about the kingdom of God" (Acts 1:3). However, they still didn't quite get it.

Read Matthew 28:17 and Acts 1:6.

Although Jesus had spent time with His followers since His resurrection trying to help them understand what He was up to, some still struggled. When He met them in Galilee there were some still doubting what had taken place. And then on the Mount of Olives, they had questions. Though Jesus clearly told His friends that He would be leaving and they'd no longer see Him (John 16:10), they still wanted to know if He was about to restore Israel's political power. Perhaps their question was motivated by the thought that, as His closest friends, He would set them up with roles of authority in this newly established kingdom. They didn't yet see the big picture, and they didn't fully understand what Jesus was doing.

We can be quick to scoff at these thick-headed disciples, but I want you to put yourself in their shoes for a moment. They had sat under this Man's teaching for a few years now. They'd heard Him talk about the kingdom of God, and how it was near. They'd seen Him perform signs and wonders, heal the sick, and call the dead to rise. They aligned themselves with an outcast when both the ruling authorities of the Romans and the Jews grew hostile toward Him. They watched those authorities kill Him in the most brutal way possible. They sat in the hopelessness of their grief for three days, and then suddenly He started appearing to them in houses and talking to them alongside the road. It's no surprise that they were maybe a little confused. But they were probably also anxious to see Jesus enthroned, for power to be restored to God's people, for all the wrong things to be made right, and for Him to put His accusers in their place.

Are we really any different from them?

Have you ever felt the sin-sickness that comes from living in this fallen world and thought, *Jesus, come quickly*? Have you been wronged and desperately longed for justice to be served, for the person who hurt you to be punished and put in their place? Explain.

How did these feelings keep you from seeing the bigger picture of God's mission for this earth?

Read Matthew 28:18-20.

Instead of rebuking them for their doubts, what did Jesus do?

Jesus reminded them of who He is ("All authority has been given to me in heaven and on earth …"), gave them a new purpose ("Go … and make disciples"), and reminded them they were not alone ("I am with you always, to the end of the age").

Read Acts 1:7-11.

How did Jesus respond to their question?

He rebuked their concerns about political status and told them it was not their job to worry about what was going to happen because God is in control. Instead, He promised them they would receive an even greater power, not for their own gain but to be His witnesses throughout the whole world.

Then they stood in awe as He was taken up in a cloud into heaven and two messengers of God suddenly appeared at their side.

What did the angels say to Jesus' friends? Write Acts 1:11 in your own words.

The angels asked the disciples why they were staring after their departed friend. In his commentary on the Book of Acts, James Boice writes this about the angels' question:

> It was a way of saying, Why are you just standing here? There is work to do. Get on with it. Then the angels have a great promise: 'This same Jesus, who has been taken from you into heaven, will come back in the same way you have seen him go'… when the disciples

were told that 'this same Jesus' would be coming back, they would have thought of the Jesus they loved ... this gentle, loving, gracious but sovereign, holy, and majestic Jesus who would come back. He would stand with them and would say, Well, brothers, how have you done? What have you accomplished during all these years that I have left you to carry out my Great Commission? ... The disciples, as they thought of Jesus' return, would have been encouraged for the task at hand.[3]

When I read about the disciples gazing longingly for their friend, I think of my son saying goodbye to his papa. Like my son, Jesus' friends may have experienced the mixed emotions of aching for His physical presence while finding comfort in the promise of a future reunion. Luke wrote that they returned to Jerusalem "with great joy" after Jesus departed (Luke 24:52). They were compelled by the future promise of His return to pursue the task He purposed for them: go and tell.

In writing about the growth of the early church in Acts, Boice comments, "Every Christian—not just a formal order of missionaries ... —considered it his or her obligation to bear witness."[4]

You and I have the same promise and purpose as Jesus' friends did so many years ago. Like them, we have been commissioned to bear witness to what He has done in our lives and to make disciples. The promise of His return should compel us to complete the task.

How are you currently doing with your assignment, sisters?

celebrate
Easter

by Larissa Arnault Roach

Easter is a time for our biggest celebration. Let the world see the hope of Christ in you as you welcome others around your table.

Easter is one of the easiest times to invite others who might not know what they believe, regularly attend church, or understand why we celebrate. Because we are Easter people, we long to share the hope of Christ with others. For this reason, in the space below, write down the names of three people (or families) in your life who are unchurched to pray for. Not just three people you know, but three people who are actively in your life—including friends, family members, coworkers, or neighbors.

1.

2.

3.

(If you struggled to come up with three people, ask God to bring these people into your life and seek opportunities to venture outside your comfort zone.) Pray for these people by name, but also try to enter daily life with them. Don't judge them and don't make them a project. Just love them and build relationships with them.

On Easter Sunday, host a lunch and invite these three families to join you. Consider inviting other believers to the meal. Let this be a time of connection and fun. Inviting people in for a meal is an easy way to build relationships. Plus, people who might be reluctant to attend a church service will not be so intimidated by a meal at a friend's home.

Here are some ideas for the centerpiece to your table:

1. Monochromatic. Pick one color and buy lots of different kinds of flowers for one impressive arrangement. This takes the guesswork out of what goes together! A big bunch of white tulips, lilies, rosebuds, carnations, and daisies looks stunning when the flowers are all in the same tone.

2. Herbs. Gather bunches of herbs to display in small vases, mason jars, or terra-cotta pots that will fill the room with the fresh scent of spring. Place containers of rosemary, mint, chives, and thyme down a line in the center of the table. Keep arrangements low to the table to provide open space above for conversations to flow.

3. Berry baskets. If you've whipped up a berry pie or tart for the occasion, reuse the baskets the berries came in as centerpiece vessels. Pack each container with cut flowers, cutting the stems short so there is a fullness to the basket. Display on a cake plate to add height.

live boldly
for Christ

by Amanda Mejias

"Death has been swallowed up in victory. Where, death, is your victory? Where, death, is your sting?" (1 Cor. 15:54b-55). He is alive!

Yes, Jesus is alive! No grave could keep Him down. The curse of death has been broken. Sin has been declared powerless, and we get to sing our praises to a living God.

So what happens when we believe this? What does this change about the way we live for Christ? The answer should be: Everything!

Read Matthew 28:18-20 with your teen. After you finish reading, take time to consider and both list what you would do for Christ if you knew you wouldn't fail or experience disapproval from others. Your list could include things such as sharing the gospel with a coworker or classmate, going on a mission trip, or inviting your neighbors to church, and so on.

Here's the deal. If this command had been given to us before Jesus was resurrected, we would have lacked two things to carry it out: His power and His presence. It was because of His resurrection that He declared, "All authority has been given to me in heaven and on earth" (v. 18).

It is why He was able to say, "Remember, I am with you always, to the end of the age" (v. 20). And because we have His power and presence, we are able to confidently go into the world, or across the street, or into the classroom and make disciples. Because of what He's done, we can boldly live for Him.

Discuss with your teen how the assurance of Jesus' presence and power changes the way you view the tasks on the list you made. Pray together and ask God to give you boldness this week as you strive to obey His command from Matthew 28.

If your teen does not yet have a relationship with Christ, you have the privilege of being the example of a vibrant Christian. Take the lead on this week's activity and make known the God of your salvation!

share God's love
this Easter

by Kayla Stevens

Jesus' obedience to God the Father and His love for us compelled Him to suffer and die for our sins, and rise again on the third day to defeat death and the grave. The true story of Easter is too important not to share.

GATHER

- Construction paper
- Markers or crayons
- Glue
- Glitter, sequins, and other fun adornments

Jesus appeared to many of His disciples after the resurrection and told them to tell others the good news of the gospel and make disciples. The same commission Jesus gave His disciples applies to us today. As we celebrate Easter, we have unique opportunities to share this good news with others, including our friends and neighbors.

With your kids, make "Happy Easter" cards to distribute to your neighbors. Include a personal message and Easter Scripture reference in each card (such as Matt. 28:5-6 or Mark 16:5-6). Also consider including a fun Easter treat to deliver along with your card. As you create your Easter cards, pray for God to give you opportunities to build relationships with your neighbors and share God's love with them. As a family, deliver your cards and treats to your neighbors.

After you deliver your cards and treats, talk to your kids about the importance of sharing God's love with others. Schedule a time together each week as a family to pray for some of your neighbors, asking God to give you more opportunities to get to know them and share God's love with them.

Beyond the Resurrection

Looking to the Horizon

by Sarah Doss

As we read last week in Acts 1, Jesus told His followers what they would do next. He said, "You will receive power when the Holy Spirit has come on you, and you will be my witnesses in Jerusalem, in all Judea and Samaria, and to the ends of the earth" (v. 8).

Then, the Bible says Jesus "was taken up as they were watching, and a cloud took him out of their sight" (Acts 1:9). I have so many follow-up questions about this event, but we'll have to shelve those for another day. The apostles who had been listening to Jesus speak were staring into heaven. I imagine they were, understandably, a little baffled at what they'd just witnessed and were trying to make some sense of it. Though, these were some of the guys who'd learned from Jesus for years, so maybe they were more accustomed to miracles than we are. But it still seems to have come as a shock to them.

Next we're told that men in white robes showed up and said, "Men of Galilee, why do you stand looking up into heaven? This same Jesus, who has been taken from you into heaven, will come in the same way that you have seen him going into heaven" (Acts 1:11).

And, just like that, Jesus was gone.

But, did you notice the hope we're left with? Just as Jesus did with His followers when He rose from the dead—in His ascension, He provided purpose and peace for His disciples. He told them the same Holy Spirit who was coming to comfort and guide them would also empower them to carry the gospel to the world. That Spirit is now at work in us!

Also, just moments after Jesus was taken up into heaven, messengers reassured His followers that He would return. That hope is also ours!

We find the promise of Christ's return over and over in Scripture (for example, see 1 Thess. 4:16). He is coming back. We know Jesus will return to claim His Bride and to make all things new, restoring heaven and earth and allowing us to live in communion with Him forever. In Revelation 22:7 (ESV) Jesus says, "Behold, I am coming soon."

With the assurance that Jesus has not left us alone and that He's coming back soon to set the world right, where does that leave us for now?

We've been given the all-important assignment of showing "the surpassing value of knowing Christ Jesus" (Phil. 3:8) to the rest of the world who doesn't know Him.

We're tasked with being His witnesses, in ever-expanding circles. Basically, He wants us to tell everyone who He is and what He has done to give us access to God. To borrow some New Testament phrasing from Paul, we have the joy of being ministers of reconciliation—telling people that God loves them and wants to be in relationship with them, showing them the joy that comes from knowing God. Paul says, "Therefore, we are ambassadors for Christ, since God is making his appeal through us. We plead on Christ's behalf, 'Be reconciled to God.' He made the one who did not know sin to be sin for us, so that in him we might become the righteousness of God" (2 Cor. 5:20-21).

Remember the St. Augustine quote we read at the beginning of our study? He said, "We are Easter people and alleluia is our song."[1] I wonder if you read that quote differently now than you did when we began our study together.

With the purpose and hope that Jesus has placed in our hearts and lives as His redeemed children, we each sing our own unique alleluias and arias of praise as we walk in step with Him, abiding and obeying, repenting and realigning, giving Him glory and feeling the joy and security of being a cherished daughter—one our good Father delights in. In light of these beautiful realities, I want my life to be marked by thankful praise. What about you?

What alleluia will you sing today?

What was your favorite day of study this past week? Why?

What were some of your emotions as you studied about the resurrection this week?

How have you experienced Jesus meeting you exactly where you are and caring for you in your grief, hurt, and pain?

Have you ever struggled to believe the resurrection actually took place? Explain. If someone were to ask you why the resurrection is such a big deal, what would you say?

How are you currently carrying out the Great Commission? What's difficult and challenging about making disciples? How have you experienced the Holy Spirit empowering you to be a witness?

Do you believe Jesus' return is imminent, causing you to live your life with urgency? Or do you see it as something that will take place out there in the future, with little effect on your life now? Explain.

What is your biggest takeaway from this Easter study? How has it changed the way you approach this Easter season? How has it affected the way you live your life for Christ?

ENDNOTES

INTRODUCTION

1. William H. Shannon, *Silence on Fire: The Prayer of Awareness* (Crossroad Pub., 1993), 146.

WEEK 1

1. Jared M. August, "The Messianic Hope of Genesis: The Protoevangelium and Patriarchal Promises, " Retrieved from https://themelios.thegospelcoalition.org/article/the-messianic-hope-of-genesis-the-protoevangelium-and-patriarchal-promises/) (Vol. 42, Issue 1).

2. Douglas K. Stuart, *New American Commentary Vol 02: Exodus.* (Nashville: B&H Publishing Group, 2012). Retrieved from https://app.wordsearchbible.lifeway.com.

3. Bruce Corley, Steve W. Lemke, and Grant I. Lovejoy, *Biblical Hermenuetics: A Comprehensive Introduction to Interpreting Scripture, second edition.* (Nashville: B&H Publishing Group, 2002).

WEEK 2

1. Annie Dillard. https://www.brainpickings.org/2013/06/07/annie-dillard-the-writing-life-1/.

2. Max Anders and Stuart K. Weber, *HNTC Vol. 01: Matthew.* (Nashville: B&H Publishing Group, 2012). Retrieved from https://app.wordsearchbible.lifeway.com.

3. Robby Gallaty, *The Forgotten Jesus* (Zondervan, 2017), 148.

4. Rick Warren, *The Purpose Driven Life* (Zondervan, 2007), 265.

5. Merrill F. Unger and R.K. Harrison, *The New Unger's Bible Dictionary, hallel.* (Moody Publishers, 2009), 178.

WEEK 3

1. Max Anders and Trent C. Butler, *HNTC Vol. 03: Luke.* (Nashville: B&H Publishing Group, 2012). Retrieved from https://app.wordsearchbible.lifeway.com.

2. "Roman Crucifixion Mythods Reveal the History of Crucifixion," Biblical Archaeology Society. Retrieved from https://www.biblicalarchaeology.org/daily/biblical-topics/crucifixion/roman-crucifixion-methods-reveal-the-history-of-crucifixion/.

3. Andreas Köstenberger, L. Scott Kellum, and Charles L. Quarles, *The Cradle, the Cross, and the Crown: An Introduction to the New Testament, Second Edition.* (Nashville: B&H Academic, 2016). Retrieved from https://app.wordsearchbible.com.

WEEK 4

1. "Pearl Harbor bombed," HISTORY, Retrieved from https://www.history.com/this-day-in-history/pearl-harbor-bombed.

2. Jim Stovall, "FDR, the editor: A date which will live in infamy." Retrieved from http://www.jprof.com/2013/12/07/fdr-the-editor-a-date-which-will-live-in-infamy/.

3. James M. Boice, *Acts: An Expositional Commentary*, (Grand Rapids: Baker Books, 1997), 20.

4. Ibid, Boice, 22.

WEEK 5

1. William H. Shannon, *Silence on Fire: The Prayer of Awareness*, (Crossroad Pub., 1993),146.

KAILEY BLACK

Kailey Black serves as Content Specialist for LifeWay Leadership at LifeWay Christian Resources. She holds a Master of Christian Studies from Union University and has experience in editing, content development, and project management. Kailey and her husband, Devin, live in the Nashville area with their two children.

PAIGE CLAYTON

Paige Clayton is the Events Destination Manager for LifeWay. Prior to her work at LifeWay, Paige worked for the Operation Christmas Child project with Samaritan's Purse. She is currently finishing up a master's in professional counseling. In her spare time, she is a fun aunt to four young adult nieces and mom to her dog, Ruby. She loves traveling to places she has never been, singing, and spending time outdoors and with her family.

DEBBIE DICKERSON

Debbie Dickerson and her husband, Steve, love spending time with their oldest son, Landon, and his wife, Alyssa, and their college-aged son, Kaden. Debbie enjoys serving as editor of *Mature Living* and as a children's teacher at ClearView Baptist Church in Franklin, Tennessee.

SARAH DOSS

Sarah Doss is the Team Leader for LifeWay Women's Bible study team. With an educational background in communications from the University of Georgia, this Georgia peach now calls Nashville, Tennessee home. In her spare time, Sarah enjoys watching quirky sitcoms, a strong cup of coffee, and travel (international or otherwise).

RACHEL FORREST

Rachel Forrest is a writer who desires to tell the truth as beautifully as she can. She lives in Oklahoma with her husband and two children. She has an MA in Theological Studies and works for LifeWay as an eBook Developer. You can find her online at www.rachelleaforrest.com.

ASHLEY MARIVITTORI GORMAN

Ashley Marivittori Gorman serves as an acquisitions editor at B&H Publishing Group, an imprint of LifeWay Christian Resources. She is currently completing her MDiv from Southeastern Theological Seminary. Her passions are biblical literacy, discipleship, foster care, theology, and books. Ashley and her husband, Cole, live in Nashville, Tennessee, with their daughter Charlie.

MICHELLE R. HICKS

Michelle R. Hicks is the managing editor for *Journey* devotional magazine with LifeWay Women. Michelle served as a freelance writer, campus minister, and corporate chaplain before coming to LifeWay to minister with the event and publishing teams. She is a graduate of the University of North Texas and Southwestern Baptist Theological Seminary.

SUSAN HILL

Susan Hill is a writer, Bible teacher, and full-time editor at LifeWay. She is the author of *Dangerous Prayers: 50 Powerful Prayers That Changed the World*, as well as numerous devotional books. She and her husband, John, live near Nashville, Tennessee, with two unruly Goldendoodles.

ELIZABETH HYNDMAN

Elizabeth Hyndman reads, writes, and tweets. Officially, she's a social media strategist at LifeWay. She managed to find a job where she uses both her English undergraduate and her seminary graduate degrees every day. Elizabeth grew up in Nashville, sips chai lattes every chance she can get, and believes everyone should have a "funny picture" pose at the ready. Follow her on Twitter or Instagram at @edhyndman.

KELLY D. KING

Kelly D. King is the manager of Magazines/Devotional Publishing and Women's Ministry Training for LifeWay Christian Resources. She is the cohost of LifeWay's Marked podcast and is the author of *Ministry to Women: The Essential Guide to Leading Women in the Local Church*. She holds a Master of Theology degree from Gateway Seminary and while Nashville is where she lives, she still claims Oklahoma as her home.

BETSY LANGMADE

Betsy Langmade serves as manager for Adult Live Events at LifeWay Christian Resources. She's a mom and grandmother to her growing family and has been married to David for forty-three years. When she's not traveling or working, she enjoys her downtime outside and making memories with the family.

AMANDA MEJIAS

Amanda Mejias serves as the LifeWay Girls Brand Specialist, and she is passionate about equipping church leaders as they minister to and disciple teen girls. Amanda feels like she is living a dream, especially with her husband and their daughter at her side. She is also always down to hear a cheesy joke, grab coffee, and talk about golden retrievers. Amanda holds her master's degree from Liberty University's Rawlings School of Divinity.

TESSA MORRELL

Tessa Morrell is a production editor for ongoing curriculum at LifeWay. An Illinois native, she has called Nashville home for ten years now. She is passionate about serving in her local church and studying the Word of God with others in Bible study. When she's not busy reading, she enjoys visiting local coffee shops, spending hours browsing in antique stores, and crafting and creating art.

CONNIA NELSON

Connia Nelson is a ministry, business, and customer-focused leader currently serving as Senior Vice President and the chief human resources officer at LifeWay Christian Resources. Connia is a transformational HR leader, trusted advisor, and change agent. Connia currently leads a woman's community group at Rolling Hills Community Church in Franklin, Tennessee.

AMANDA OZMENT

Amanda Ozment is a Corgi mom and a super aunt. She is an Arkansas native and loves to "Call the Hogs" on Saturdays in the fall. She's served churches in Texas, Arkansas, and Arizona and now calls Nashville, Tennessee home.

LARISSA ARNAULT ROACH

Larissa Arnault Roach is the Marketing Manager for LifeWay Women. She loves butter, books, and bright lipstick. Always up for a special meal—Easter or otherwise— she considers Ecclesiastes 2:24-25 her life verse. Larissa lives in downtown Nashville with her husband, Nate, daughter Eliza, son Ozark, and dog Margot.

RACHEL SHAVER

Rachel Shaver works with all the books at LifeWay by day, and by night wrangles three sweet, rowdy kids—she affectionately refers to them as the "toddler mafia." She and her husband, Evan, make their home in a little town right outside Nashville, Tennessee.

AMANDA MAE STEELE

Amanda Mae Steele is a writer, photographer, and performing artist based in Franklin, Tennessee. She lives with her husband, Nick, and their 11-year-old "puppy," Dino. She is passionate about God's Word, other cultures, and sharing the gospel mostly through silly (but relatable) personal anecdotes. She serves as the B&H Kids Marketing Specialist at LifeWay.

KAYLA STEVENS

Kayla Stevens is the Content Editor for LifeWay Kids Discipleship. She is a graduate of Southeastern Baptist Theological Seminary and William Carey University. Kayla lives in Nashville, Tennessee and has served in Kids ministry for over 10 years.

BEKAH STONEKING

Bekah Stoneking serves as the Research Specialist and Content Editor for Explore the Bible: Kids at LifeWay. She holds a Master of Arts from Southeastern Baptist Theological Seminary and is currently completing her doctoral dissertation on mind, brain, and education research, also at SEBTS. She lives in Nashville, Tennessee, and teaches first and second graders at The Church at Avenue South.

ELLEN VEST

Ellen Vest is a Nashville native, wife, mom, and cheese dip enthusiast.

SAVANNAH IVEY WARD

Savannah Ivey Ward is an event project coordinator for LifeWay's Adult Live Events Team. She was born and raised in Knoxville, Tennesse, where she attended the University of Tennessee. Her background is in Women's Ministry and Communication, and she is passionate about helping women know Jesus. She loves conversation with friends, road trips, and music. Savannah and her husband, Blake, live in Nashville.

MARY WILEY

Mary Wiley is the author of *Everyday Theology*, a Bible study exploring what we believe and why it matters in our daily lives. She holds an MA in theological studies from The Southern Baptist Theological Seminary. She and her husband, John, have two kids who keep them on their toes. She works with B&H Publishing Group and hosts the Questions Kids Ask podcast. You can follow her on social @marycwiley.

CHRISTINA ZIMMERMAN

Christina Zimmerman works at LifeWay Christian Resources as the content editor for the YOU Bible study curriculum. She and her husband, Harry, currently attend Faith United Baptist Church where she serves as a Christian Education leader. Christina often has the opportunity to speak at various women's and Christian education conferences. In her spare time, she is writing her first book, which is set to release this year.

40 DAY READING PLAN

To help focus your heart this Easter season, we've created this forty day Scripture reading plan. We encourage you to start this plan thirty days before Easter.

Part 1: Looking Forward

Day 1: Genesis 3:1-15

Day 2: Genesis 49:8-12

Day 3: Exodus 12:1-13

Day 4: Numbers 21:4-9

Day 5: Deuteronomy 18:15-18

Day 6: Job 19:23-27

Day 7: Psalm 16

Day 8: Psalm 22

Day 9: Psalm 132:11-18

Day 10: Isaiah 53

Part 2: The Road to the Cross

Day 1: Luke 2:25-38

Day 2: Luke 9:51-62

Day 3: Matthew 16:13-28

Day 4: Matthew 17:1-23

Day 5: Luke 19:1-10

Day 6: Matthew 20:17-28

Day 7: Mark 11

Day 8: Matthew 21:28–22:14

Day 9: Matthew 24

Day 10: Mark 14:3-11

Part 3: The Final Days

Day 1: Luke 22:7-34

Day 2: John 13:1-28

Day 3: John 14:1-17; 15:26–16:15

Day 4: John 17

Day 5: Matthew 26:36-56

Day 6: Luke 22:54–23:22

Day 7: John 19:1-16

Day 8: Luke 23:26-43

Day 9: John 19:23-37

Day 10: Matthew 27:57-66

Part 4: The Ministry Continues

EASTER: Luke 24:1-35

Day 2: John 20:19-29

Day 3: John 21: 1-19

Day 4: Matthew 28:16-20

Day 5: Acts 1:1-14

Day 6: Acts 2

Day 7: Romans 8

Day 8: Ephesians 2

Day 9: Hebrews 11:1-6, 32–12:2

Day 10: Revelation 21:1-8; 22:16-20

Romans 10:17 says, "So faith comes from what is heard, and what is heard comes through the message about Christ."

Maybe you've stumbled across new information in this study. Or maybe you've attended church all your life, but something you read here struck you differently than it ever has before. If you have never accepted Christ but would like to, read on to discover how you can become a Christian.

Your heart tends to run from God and rebel against Him. The Bible calls this *sin*. Romans 3:23 says, "For all have sinned and fall short of the glory of God."

Yet God loves you and wants to save you from sin, to offer you a new life of hope. John 10:10b says, "I have come so that they may have life and have it in abundance."

To give you this gift of salvation, God made a way through His Son, Jesus Christ. Romans 5:8 says, "But God proves his own love for us in that while we were still sinners, Christ died for us."

You receive this gift by faith alone. Ephesians 2:8-9 says, "For you are saved by grace through faith, and this not from yourselves; it is God's gift—not from works, so that no one can boast."

Faith is a decision of your heart demonstrated by the actions of your life. Romans 10:9 says, "If you confess with your mouth, 'Jesus is Lord,' and believe in your heart that God raised him from the dead, you will be saved."

If you trust that Jesus died for your sins and want to receive new life through Him, pray a prayer similar to the following to express your repentance and faith in Him:

"DEAR GOD, I KNOW I AM A SINNER. I BELIEVE JESUS DIED TO FORGIVE ME OF MY SINS. I ACCEPT YOUR OFFER OF ETERNAL LIFE. THANK YOU FOR FORGIVING ME OF ALL MY SINS. THANK YOU FOR MY NEW LIFE. FROM THIS DAY FORWARD, I WILL CHOOSE TO FOLLOW YOU."

If you have trusted Jesus for salvation, please share your decision with your group leader or another Christian friend. If you are not already attending church, find one in which you can worship and grow in your faith. Following Christ's example, ask to be baptized as a public expression of your faith.

LET'S BE FRIENDS!

BLOG

We're here to help you grow in your faith, develop as a leader, and find encouragement as you go.

LifeWayWomen.com

SOCIAL

Find inspiration in the in-between moments of life.

@LifeWayWomen

NEWSLETTER

Be the first to hear about new studies, events, giveaways, and more by signing up.

LifeWay.com/WomensNews

LifeWay | Women